Risse/Haller/Harbst/Schramke

International Arbitration 10x10

INTERNATIONAL ARBITRATION 10x10

100 facts an in-house counsel needs to know

EDITORS AND AUTHORS

Jörg Risse • Heiko Haller
Ragnar Harbst • Jürgen Schramke

AUTHORS

Markus Altenkirch
Tobias Höfling
Annette Keilmann
Gerrit Niehoff
Max Oehm
Maximilian Sattler

2022

BECK • HART • NOMOS

Published by
Verlag C.H. Beck oHG, Wilhelmstraße 9, 80801 München, Germany,
eMail: bestellung@beck.de

Co-published by
Hart Publishing, Kemp House, Chawley Park, Cumnor Hill, Oxford, OX2 9PH, United Kingdom,
online at: www.hartpub.co.uk

and

Nomos Verlagsgesellschaft mbH & Co. KG Waldseestraße 3–5, 76530 Baden-Baden, Germany, eMail: nomos@nomos.de

Published in North America by Hart Publishing,
An Imprint of Bloomsbury Publishing 1385 Broadway, New York, NY 10018, USA

ISBN 978 3 406 77971 8 (C.H.BECK)
ISBN 978 1 5099 5723 1 (HART)
ISBN 978 3 8487 8971 9 (NOMOS)

Printed in Germany by
Beltz Grafische Betriebe GmbH
Am Fliegerhorst 8, 99947 Bad Langensalza
Typeset by
Fotosatz Buck
Zweikirchener Straße 7, 84036 Kumhausen
Cover: Kunst oder Reklame, München, based on a design by Emil Holthausen

CO_2 neutral
chbeck.de/nachhaltig

ABOUT THIS BOOK

This is a book for you, dear in-house counsel. In-house counsel are generalists. In-house counsel need concise, accurate advice about special areas of law. In-house counsel are interested in substance, not in footnotes. In-house counsel lack the time to study academic treatises and lengthy court decisions. In-house counsel look for quick orientation and easy access to key information. All this is understood. That is why this book addresses 10 x 10 different topics subdivided in 10 main chapters. That is why each topic is explained in straightforward language on exactly two pages, without "ifs" and "buts" and, of course, without footnotes. That is why you, dear in-house counsel, will invest five minutes max. of reading time to get a basic, but accurate understanding of an otherwise difficult legal topic. That is the concept, the promise of this book.

This is a book for you, dear external counsel. External counsel are specialists. External counsel are hired because they already have an in-depth knowledge of a special area of law. External counsel will not learn much by reading just another book about their area of expertise. To this end, this book may make no difference. What external counsel often need is a concise summary of their knowledge which they can share on short notice with their clients requesting information on a particular topic. External counsel are rarely paid for summarizing their vast knowledge on the requested topic in an easy-to-digest format. All this is understood. This is why this book addresses 10 x 10 different topics clients are often interested in. This is why each topic is explained in such a way that it can be shared with a client promptly to satisfy the client's initial interest. That is why you, dear external counsel, will invest five minutes max. to scan the two-page explanation of the topic and mail it to your client. That is the concept, the promise of this book.

This is a book about international arbitration. Arbitration is the dispute resolution mechanism of choice for most cross-border disputes. Arbitration is a complicated, multi-layered area of law. A transnational practice has developed, impacted by civil and common law features. At the same time, international arbitration is not rocket science. It is possible to explain 10 x 10 key concepts of international arbitration accurately and understandably on two pages each. That is a challenge, but it is doable. We have done it. This is the concept, the promise of this book.

Frankfurt/Main, Germany, in April 2022
Jörg Risse Heiko Haller Ragnar Harbst Jürgen Schramke

TABLE OF CONTENTS

I. AN INTRODUCTION TO INTERNATIONAL ARBITRATION AND OTHER ADR METHODS

(Annette Keilmann)

II. THE ARBITRATION AGREEMENT

(Tobias Höfling)

III. THE ARBITRAL TRIBUNAL

(Max Oehm)

IV. THE ARBITRAL PROCEEDINGS

(Heiko Haller)

V. TAKING OF EVIDENCE

(Ragnar Harbst)

VI. PSYCHOLOGY IN INTERNATIONAL ARBITRATION

(Jörg Risse)

VII. INTERIM MEASURES AND OTHER INTERACTIONS BETWEEN COURTS AND THE ARBITRAL TRIBUNAL

(Maximilian Sattler)

VIII. AWARDS AND ENFORCEMENT IN DOMESTIC COURTS

(Gerrit Niehoff)

I.

AN INTRODUCTION TO INTERNATIONAL ARBITRATION AND OTHER ADR METHODS

1. TALKING ABOUT ARBITRATION REQUIRES KNOWLEDGE OF SOME TERMS

Some terms will be referred to at various times throughout this book and are part of the standard vocabulary for international arbitration. The advanced reader may directly move on to the next subchapter. For those who do not frequently deal with international arbitration, it may be helpful to glance over the explanation of the terms.

NEW YORK CONVENTION (OR "NYC")

The 1958 New York Convention on the Recognition and Enforcement of Foreign Arbitral Awards ("New York Convention") is one of the most successful international conventions. At present, 169 states are party to the convention. Thereby, they are obliged to ensure that foreign awards are recognized and generally capable of enforcement in their jurisdiction. As a consequence, it is usually easier to enforce an arbitral award in a foreign country than a state court decision.

UNCITRAL MODEL LAW ("MODEL LAW")

The United Nations Commission on International Trade Law ("UNCITRAL") prepared the Model Law on International Commercial Arbitration ("Model Law") in 1985 and amended it in 2006. The Model Law is designed for use by states as a kind of template for modernizing their law of international arbitration. So far, 85 states have used the Model Law as the basis for their national arbitration laws. As a consequence, many national arbitration laws are similar.

A list of the Model Law states can be found on the UNCITRAL website (https://uncitral.un.org/en/texts/arbitration/modellaw/commercial_arbitration/status). The list shows which states have amended previous legislation based on the Model Law and which states have based their legislation on the 2006 Model Law. Germany and Singapore, for example, have implemented the Model Law with some changes. Switzerland and Sweden have not implemented the Model Law, but there are no fundamental differences in their arbitration laws. Other states which have not implemented the Model Law are France, the United Kingdom, and most of the United States.

INSTITUTIONAL ARBITRATION

If the parties have agreed on institutional arbitration, an arbitration institution administers the arbitral proceedings. Also, each institution provides a set of rules which defines the procedure for conducting the arbitration. Frequently, the institutions also provide rules for other dispute resolution methods such as adjudication or mediation. The rules of an arbitration institution apply if the parties have agreed to submit their dispute to the rules of the specific institution. In order to agree on the application of institutional arbitration under the rules of an arbitration institution, it is recommendable to use the model clause provided by the respective institution (for details see II. 4).

There is a large number of national and international arbitration institutions. Major arbitration institutions include the following (see also II. 6):

1. International Chamber of Commerce (ICC; www.iccwbo.org/dispute-resolution-services/arbitration) with the 2021 ICC Rules of Arbitration ("ICC Rules")
2. London Court of International Arbitration (LCIA; www.lcia.org) with the 2020 LCIA Arbitration Rules ("LCIA Rules")
3. Swiss Chambers' Arbitration Institution (SCAI; https://www.swissarbitration.org) with the 2021 Swiss Rules of International Arbitration ("Swiss Rules")
4. Arbitration Institute of the Stockholm Chamber of Commerce (SCC; https://sccinstitute.com) with the 2017 SCC Arbitration Rules ("SCC Rules")
5. German Arbitration Institute (DIS; www.disarb.org) with the 2018 DIS Arbitration Rules ("DIS Rules")
6. Vienna International Arbitral Centre (VIAC; www.viac.eu/en/) with the 2021 VIAC Rules of Arbitration ("Vienna Rules")
7. International Centre for Dispute Resolution (ICDR; www.icdr.org) with the 2021 International Dispute Resolution Procedures ("ICDR Rules")
8. American Arbitration Association (AAA; www.adr.org) with its 2013 Commercial Arbitration Rules ("AAA Rules")
9. Singapore International Arbitration Centre (SIAC; www.siac.org.sg) with the 2016 SIAC Rules ("SIAC Rules")
10. Hong Kong International Arbitration Centre (HKIAC; www.hkiac.org) with the 2018 HKIAC Administered Arbitration Rules ("HKIAC Rules")
11. China International Economic and Trade Arbitration Commission (CIETAC; http://www.cietac.org/?l=en) with the 2015 China International Economic and Trade Arbitration Commission (CIETAC) Arbitration Rules ("CIETAC Rules")

12. Permanent Court of Arbitration (PCA; https://pca-cpa.org) with the 2012 PCA Arbitration Rules ("PCA Rules").

AD HOC ARBITRATION / UNCITRAL ARBITRATION RULES

Ad hoc arbitration means that the arbitration is not administered by an institution. The parties conduct *ad hoc* arbitration if they agreed on arbitration without agreeing on institutional arbitration. In such a case it is left to the parties to determine all aspects of the arbitral proceedings themselves, e. g. to determine the procedure for appointing the arbitrators. The parties may, however, agree that – although no arbitration institution will be involved – an established set of rules shall nevertheless be applied.

In such a case, agreeing on the application of the UNCITRAL Arbitration Rules is a good idea because they are specifically designed for *ad hoc* arbitrations. These rules were initially adopted by the United Nations Commission on International Trade Law in 1976 and have been revised in 2010 and 2013. As UNCITRAL puts it, the UNCITRAL Rules

> "provide a comprehensive set of procedural rules upon which parties may agree for the conduct of arbitral proceedings arising out of their commercial relationship and are widely used in ad hoc arbitrations as well as administered arbitrations. The Rules cover all aspects of the arbitral process, providing a model arbitration clause, setting out procedural rules regarding the appointment of arbitrators and the conduct of arbitral proceedings, and establishing rules in relation to the form, effect and interpretation of the award."
>
> *(https://uncitral.un.org/en/texts/arbitration/contractualtexts/arbitration)*

SEAT OF ARBITRATION AND LEX ARBITRI

The seat of arbitration designates the legal domicile of an international arbitration. It refers to a specific jurisdiction (state). This means that the laws applicable to arbitration in that particular state apply to the arbitral proceedings (the so-called *lex arbitri*, i. e. the law of the arbitration; for details see IV. 8). The *lex arbitri* regulates the relationship between an arbitral tribunal and the state courts in that jurisdiction. The seat of arbitration also determines the state in which the arbitral award can be challenged before the state courts (see VIII. 1).

The seat of arbitration (which is often also referred to as the place of arbitration) must not be confused with the place in which a hearing is conducted. In principle, the place of the hearing does not matter and is independent from the legal seat of arbitration.

IBA RULES AND GUIDELINES

The International Bar Association ("IBA") has issued a number of rules and guidelines on arbitration. The most prominent in practice are the IBA Rules on the Taking of Evidence (see V. 1 for details) and the IBA Guidelines on Conflict of Interest (see III. 5 for details). The IBA rules and guidelines represent a standard of international best practice. As a consequence, arbitral tribunals will often follow the IBA rules and guidelines, even in the absence of an express agreement by the parties to do so.

COMPETENCE-COMPETENCE

According to the competence-competence doctrine, an arbitral tribunal has a preliminary competence to decide on its own jurisdiction. In other words, the tribunal – and not a state court – decides, in the first instance, whether it is competent to rule on an issue before it. However, it may ultimately be decided by a state court whether the arbitral tribunal really was competent to decide the issue. This is when an award is challenged on the grounds that the arbitral tribunal was allegedly not competent (for details see VIII. 3 and 5).

SEPARABILITY PRESUMPTION

This presumption means that an arbitration agreement is to be treated independently from the rest of the contract in which it is contained. Therefore, it is possible that the arbitration agreement is valid although the contract is not, or vice versa (for details see II. 9).

ALTERNATIVE DISPUTE RESOLUTION ("ADR")

ADR is a collective term for various out-of-court proceedings which have in common that there is no judge or any other authority deciding the dispute. Rather, the parties aim at finding a consensual solution. Mediation is probably the best-known ADR technique (see I. 3). Other ADR techniques include "Early Neutral Evaluation" (obtainment of a non-binding legal opinion) or a "Mini Trial" (simulation of court proceedings before the management of the parties to the dispute). "Arb-Med" or "Med-Arb" is a relatively new alternative dispute resolution mechanism combining arbitration and mediation (see I. 8).

2. COOPERATIVE NEGOTIATING IS NOT "FRIENDLIER" THAN COMPETITIVE NEGOTIATING

The focus of this book lies on arbitration. However, before it comes to arbitral proceedings, the parties usually try to settle their dispute by way of negotiations or a formalized process of alternative dispute resolution, for example mediation. In some instances, such attempts for an amicable solution of the dispute are mandatory before arbitral proceedings can be initiated (see II. 7).

Most lawyers are used to the so-called adversarial approach to negotiating: both parties enter into the negotiation with their maximum demand and only fight over mutual concessions. Each party, on the one hand, tries to uphold their own position (including deceiving the other party about their willingness to make concessions). On the other hand, each party seeks to diminish the other party's belief in the possibility to realize its demand. Key factors for success in competitive negotiations are information, time and negotiating power.

The problem with this approach is that negotiations may fail despite the existence of a zone within which an agreement would be possible. Such zone is called the **Z**one **O**f **P**ossible **A**greement ("ZOPA"), and it is designated as follows: a ZOPA exists if there is a zone within which both parties would prefer a negotiated agreement over a legal dispute. If the parties use a competitive negotiating strategy, it may not become apparent that an agreement is actually possible. This is because each party operates with a maximum position which may be very far away from a negotiated result the party would actually be willing to accept. Even if an agreement is reached through a competitive negotiation process, it is often the lowest common denominator so that joint gains are left on the table.

Cooperative negotiating can often avoid an undesirable outcome of this nature. This approach is based on the differentiation between positions (i. e. the request expressed) and the underlying interests. If the parties concentrate on their interests during the negotiation rather than on defending positions, this may open the way to various alternative solutions which better satisfy their interests ("win-win situation" instead of a "zero-sum situation"). Cooperative negotiating must not be confused with "soft" negotiating. This is because emphatically representing one's own interests is not "softer" than unproductively defending one's own position. Rather, the cooperative concept stands for a structurally different approach to negotiating.

The best known cooperative negotiation approach was developed at Harvard University starting in the 1970s. The results of the Harvard Negotiation Project were publicized in the bestseller "Getting to Yes" by Roger Fisher and William Ury. The guiding principles of the Harvard Concept are as follows:

- Separate the people from the problem. This means that the negotiators disentangle the problem to be solved from their personal views about their counterpart.
- Focus on interests, not positions.
- Be creative and invent options for mutual gains (without, at this step, deciding whether to pursue an option or not). This is typically called "enlarging the pie" (instead of simply "dividing the existing pie").
- Insist on using objective criteria. It is recommended that the parties first discuss and agree on the process for dividing the pie (instead of directly negotiating who gets what).
- Know your "BATNA", i.e. the **B**est **A**lternative **t**o a **N**egotiated **A**greement. The BATNA often is a better scale for evaluating one's own success in negotiations than an absolute internal limit fixed at the outset of the negotiation. A negotiated agreement is a success if its result is better than the BATNA. Knowing one's own BATNA will prevent negotiators from prematurely walking away from the negotiation table.

Some conflicts are so complex that the complexity threatens to overburden the negotiators. It is recommendable to organize the complexity by dividing the negotiation into different phases and first agreeing on the process. Simply reducing the complexity by leaving out certain aspects is only the second-best option. This may prevent the parties from finding creative solutions which better satisfy their interests. Also, negotiations are more likely to fail if the situation is not cleared up completely because the parties do not engage in a full transfer of knowledge.

Finally, psychological traps and other cognitive barriers to rational negotiation behavior endanger the success of negotiations. Such barriers include:

- Overconfidence in one's own chances of success and reactive devaluation of arguments or suggestions made by the opposing party.
- Cognitive dissonance: research shows that individuals strive to uphold and defend the once contrived vision of the world. As a consequence, information which does not tally with this vision will only be selectively perceived. This may lead to a so-called confirmation bias.
- Framing of judgements: judgements can be manipulated by framing the problem, e.g. in a positive or negative way. This can be used as a tactical device to "anchor" perceptions.
- Bias towards assuming a zero-sum situation.

3. MEDIATION IS A WELL-ESTABLISHED METHOD FOR SOLVING ECONOMIC DISPUTES

"Surely mediation is just a strange 'psycho'-technique barely suitable for resolving family conflicts, let alone 'real business' problems!?" Such an assumption can only be described as: emphatically wrong. In cases where a dispute cannot be resolved through informal negotiations, the parties may resort to a formalized process of alternative dispute resolution such as mediation. Mediation and arbitration can even be legally intertwined (see I. 8 and II. 7).

Mediation is a process by which the parties seek to settle their dispute under the guidance of a neutral third party, the mediator. Mediation is generally voluntary. However, the parties may have agreed in their dispute resolution clause that an attempt to mediate is obligatory (for details see I. 8). Also, mediation is generally private, i. e. free from state involvement (although some states have established a kind of hybrid proceeding combining state court proceedings and mediation). The purpose of mediation is to resolve a conflict focusing on the goals and interests of the parties rather than on their rights from a purely legal perspective.

Mediation has become increasingly accepted also for solving commercial disputes. There is a number of skilled mediators who also act as counsel and/or arbitrators in commercial disputes. A successful mediation can help preserve commercial relationships because it is not an adversarial process. In addition, mediation offers a chance for creative solutions. A compromise found may involve elements which could not have been part of the outcome of arbitration or state court proceedings. For example, it could be agreed that instead of paying damages, a party would grant a discount for future deliveries. Also, dispute resolution by way of mediation is less time-consuming and more cost-effective than legal proceedings.

In order to use mediation as a tool for resolving their dispute, the parties may agree that an established set of rules such as the 2014 ICC Mediation Rules shall apply. To that extent, the ICC and other institutions provide standard clauses which the parties may use for their contract. If the parties agree on these rules, the mediation is administered by the said institution, i. e. ICC mediations are administered by the ICC International Centre for ADR. However, the parties do not have to formalize the mediation in such a way. They may also simply engage a mediator and agree with him or her on the terms and the process of the mediation.

A typical mediation goes through the following phases:

Pre-Mediation Phase: drafting of the mediation agreement and preparation of the mediation session.

Opening Phase: the mediator informs the parties about the structure of the mediation and defines the rules applicable to the mediation (possibly also conclusion of a "negotiation contract" setting out the parties' agreement on the further conduct of the mediation proceedings).

Fact Finding/Information Gathering: determination of the issues to be resolved and establishment of the relevant facts.

Working Through Conflict: discussion of the subject matter and the legal situation (includes exploration of the interests underlying the defined positions; the mediator aims at working out each party's aspirations and motivations).

Developing and Evaluating Options: joint development of alternative solutions and evaluation of the same.

Final Phase: finalizing of the (partial) settlement agreement.

The mediator has full control over and is actively involved in the dispute resolution process. However, the mediator has no decision-making power. Rather, he or she structures the discussion, breaks down the issues, ranks them and frames them in a way that facilitates the resolution of the dispute by the parties involved. In addition, the mediator employs specific techniques in order to encourage a settlement. The easiest technique is using questions, e.g. to gather information, to steer the discussion or to stimulate ideas. A skilled mediator will also employ active listening. This means that the mediator verbalizes and/or rephrases statements made by the parties with the aim of gathering further information in order to get the "full picture". Also, this technique helps to make the parties feel understood.

A special tool for mediation are so-called caucuses. These are private sessions between the mediator and each party to enable the parties to speak about their interests and aspirations in confidence. This technique, however, is not without risk as it may endanger the mediator's impartiality. Another common feature of mediation processes is that the mediator puts a statement made by one party into another context or changes the point of reference (so-called reframing). The aim is to show that a party's view of the conflict is one-dimensional and that the party needs to change its perspective in order to be open for a resolution of the conflict.

4. DISPUTE ADJUDICATION BOARDS ARE A VIABLE OPTION FOR MAJOR PROJECTS

While negotiations and mediation seek to settle a dispute amicably, arbitration is a controversial dispute resolution mechanism (see I. 6). Before it comes to arbitration, the parties may try to solve their dispute through adjudication – a similarly controversial dispute resolution process. Adjudication is usually linked to international arbitration (see I. 5).

A Dispute Adjudication Board ("DAB") is a standing body which the parties have agreed to establish in order to swiftly resolve disputes that may arise between them. DABs originally evolved in the U.K. but are nowadays widespread, especially in the construction and engineering industry. The FIDIC standard forms of contract, for example, provide for the appointment of a DAB.

The DAB is usually established in the early phase of a project so that it is readily available when a dispute arises. If the parties refrain from establishing a standing body, they can nevertheless agree (before or after a dispute has arisen) that one or more adjudicators be appointed. The adjudicator(s) will then decide the dispute in the same way a standing DAB would.

A DAB (or an adjudication panel created *ad hoc*) usually consists of one or three knowledgeable independent persons chosen by the parties. Frequently, each party chooses one person (alternatively, the parties jointly choose two members), and the two members will then appoint the chairperson. The parties are well advised to agree on a fallback position in case this process does not work (e.g. appointment of the adjudicator(s) by a certain institution). Adjudicators do not necessarily have to be lawyers; they can be engineers, for example (although it may be advisable to have at least one member who is legally qualified).

The rules applicable to the adjudication proceedings are determined by the parties. They agree either on the appointment of a DAB (e.g. by using a FIDIC contract) or on adjudication and set the rules applicable to the course of the proceedings. To that extent, it is recommendable that the parties agree on the application of an established set of rules such as the 2015 ICC Dispute Board Rules. The ICC and other institutions provide standard clauses which the parties may use for their contract. In the application of institutional dispute board rules, the institution can provide administrative services to the parties. These services usually include appointing adjudicators, deciding upon challenges against adjudicators, determining the fees of the adjudicators, and possibly reviewing decisions.

All this will have to be regulated in detail by the parties if they do not agree on the application of a pre-defined set of rules for the adjudication proceedings.

Decisions of the adjudicator(s) are usually temporarily binding. This means that the parties are obliged to comply with the decision but remain free to submit the dispute to a court or to arbitration by issuing a so-called notice of dissatisfaction (for further details see I. 5). However, different from an arbitral award, a decision rendered in adjudication proceedings is not readily enforceable except in the unlikely event that the specific jurisdiction provides for enforceability. In the absence of such provisions, the adjudicator's(s') decision becomes enforceable like a contract term. However, if the other party does not comply with its contractual obligation, one would have to initiate legal proceedings in order to compel the party to comply with its obligations (= action for breach of contract). Grounds to resist enforcement may include lack of jurisdiction of the adjudicator(s) or lack of fairness.

There is an alternative to a DAB, the so-called Dispute Review Board ("DRB"). A DRB, according to the parties' agreement, only renders non-binding recommendations. Yet, the parties may agree that these recommendations also become binding if no notice of dissatisfaction is sent to the other party within a specified time limit.

As adjudication is available on short notice when a dispute arises, it constitutes a valuable tool for contemporary evaluation of a dispute. Immediate resolution of disputes (at least with temporarily binding effect) is of the essence – especially in construction projects where there is a risk that the construction process may be interrupted because of disputes. Moreover, adjudication may save costs for arbitration or litigation if the decision is accepted by the parties. However, since the costs of a standing body are relatively high, DABs are less attractive for small projects.

5. ADJUDICATION IS USUALLY LINKED TO INTERNATIONAL ARBITRATION

A decision rendered in adjudication proceedings (see I. 4) is usually binding if and as long as the dispute has not been settled or decided by a court/an arbitral tribunal. This means that a party disagreeing with the outcome of the adjudication may refer the dispute to litigation or arbitration. Whether state courts or an arbitral tribunal have the last word depends on the dispute resolution clause the parties have agreed on. If an arbitration agreement has been concluded, the dispute may finally be resolved through arbitration. In the absence of an arbitration agreement, the dispute can be litigated before the competent state courts. The standard dispute adjudication clauses, however, regularly provide for arbitration.

The arbitral tribunal (or the court) is not bound by the adjudicator's(s') decision. Also, the tribunal or court does not decide whether this decision was correct or not. Rather, it decides independently on the merits of the case. But what happens if the court/arbitral tribunal comes to a different decision? Is a party who has acted in accordance with the adjudicator's(s') decision possibly liable for damages incurred by the other side? It is advisable to include provisions to that extent in the contract, for example by reference to institutional adjudication rules. The German DIS Adjudication Rules, e. g., provide that a party who, relying on the binding effect of a decision, has carried out or refrained from carrying out legal acts in accordance with this decision is not obligated to pay damages to the other party.

If neither party notifies the other party about its dissatisfaction with the adjudicator's(s') decision within the contractually stipulated time limit, the decision will become final and binding upon the parties. An exception to the rule "temporarily binding effect" may be considered if the decision is manifestly incorrect. The DIS Adjudication Rules, for example, provide that non-compliance with a decision rendered in adjudication proceedings shall not be sanctioned in cases where the proceedings suffered from a defect which in corresponding arbitral proceedings would lead to the setting aside of an award according to the German Code of Civil Procedure.

The conduct of adjudication proceedings can be a necessary precondition for arbitration (or state court litigation) to be admissible. Whether this is the case or not depends on the parties' agreement. When drafting a dispute resolution clause which includes different steps in the process such as adjudication and arbitration, special care has to be taken (see I. 8). The standard dispute adjudication board clauses frequently provide that the dispute shall first be adjudicated and can only move to the next step in the dispute resolution process if the adjudication fails. If a party nevertheless wishes to "bypass" the adjudication and the other party objects, an arbitral tribunal (or court) would not have jurisdiction or would dismiss the claims as – for the time being – unfounded (depending on the view in the respective jurisdiction). The conduct of the adjudication proceedings is therefore in principle a necessary precondition for initiating arbitration/litigation. Yet, also in this case, there are situations in which a decision in the adjudication proceeding is not required before referring the dispute to arbitration/litigation. These are, most notably, the following:

- The adjudicator's(s') decision is not rendered within the foreseen timeframe.
- The DAB disbanded before the dispute arose.
- A party does not comply with the adjudicator's(s') decision which has become finally binding. In this case, the other party may directly resort to a tribunal and enforce the decision. There is no need to involve the previous adjudicator(s) again.

6. INTERNATIONAL ARBITRATION IS NEITHER AMICABLE NOR NON-BINDING

Lawyers, at least in non-English speaking countries, frequently have to explain to non-lawyers that an arbitrator is not the same as a referee in sports. They must also explain that arbitration has nothing to do with a "soft" or informal procedure to find an amicable settlement. Rather, arbitration is a way of obtaining a binding and final decision in a dispute without requiring a decision in a state court. Arbitration is the principal dispute resolution mechanism in international trade. One of the reasons for this is that one party often fears a disadvantage should a dispute be dealt with by the state courts in the other party's home country. Instead, the parties refer their dispute to one or more arbitrators, who are private individuals. The arbitral award takes the place of a final and binding decision by a state court. Arbitration is based on party autonomy. It is not the coercive power of any state which would grant an arbitral tribunal the authority to decide the parties' dispute. Rather, arbitral awards are binding on the parties because the parties have agreed to it.

The arbitrators decide the dispute in accordance with the applicable legal rules. There is a whole set of laws and rules which apply to international arbitration. First of all, there is the law that determines whether a valid arbitration agreement has been concluded. Then, there may be mandatory provisions of the state in which the arbitration is seated concerning the arbitral procedure and the interaction with state courts in that country. In addition, the parties may have agreed on the applicability of further rules for the conduct of the proceedings (for further details see I. 7).

If the parties have agreed on institutional arbitration, an arbitration institution such as the ICC or the LCIA administers the arbitration process. Also, each institution provides a set of rules which defines the procedure for conducting the arbitration. These rules apply if the parties have agreed to submit their dispute to the rules of the specific arbitration institution, either already in the arbitration agreement or later on. If the parties have agreed on arbitration without the involvement of an arbitration institution, they conduct a so-called *ad hoc* arbitration. In such a case, it is left to the parties to determine all aspects of the arbitration procedure themselves, e.g. the procedure for appointing the arbitrators. However, the parties may agree that – although no arbitration institution is involved – an established set of rules shall nevertheless be applied. The UNCITRAL Arbitration Rules, for example, are specifically designed for *ad hoc* arbitrations. As explained below (II. 5), institutional arbitration is preferable to *ad hoc* arbitration.

If the parties have concluded a valid arbitration agreement and at least one party insists on arbitration, the respective dispute can no longer be submitted to the state courts for resolution. In other words, an arbitration agreement excludes the jurisdiction of the state courts. Therefore, a state court will refer the parties to arbitration unless it finds that there is no valid arbitration agreement. Also, if the dispute has been validly referred to arbitration, there is no appeal to a state court. Yet, one party could try to set aside an arbitral award before a state court. Grounds for setting aside are, however, limited. In particular, there is no second review of the merits of the case. Rather, under the national arbitration law, the state court is usually restricted to examining whether (i) the matter was covered by the arbitration agreement, (ii) the minimum requirements of due process were complied with, and (iii) the arbitral award is not in conflict with public policy (for details see VIII.).

State courts also come into play when an arbitral award needs to be enforced, i. e. when the losing party does not comply with the arbitral tribunal's decision. This is because the enforcement of a decision involves the exercise of sovereign authority. However, the state court is not a "second instance" here either. Rather, like in setting-aside proceedings, the court is generally restricted to examining whether (i) the matter was validly submitted to arbitration, (ii) the elementary rules of due process were not violated, and (iii) the enforcement of the award is not contrary to public policy. In practice, the recognition and enforcement of foreign awards are governed by the New York Convention to which more than 160 states have acceded. Therefore, in most countries of the world, the enforcement of a foreign arbitral award is easier than the enforcement of a decision of a foreign state court (for details see VIII.).

7. ARBITRATION DOES NOT TAKE PLACE IN A LEGAL VACUUM

It is a common misunderstanding – especially among non-lawyers – that arbitration takes places in a kind of legal vacuum. However, there are multiple conventions, laws and rules which make international arbitration possible.

First, there is the national arbitration law. These are the statutes which set the ground rules for arbitral proceedings seated in the respective state. The mandatory provisions of the law of the seat of arbitration are the only rules that necessarily apply to the arbitral proceedings. The national arbitration laws usually cover the arbitral process from the conclusion of an arbitration agreement, the composition and jurisdiction of the arbitral tribunal through to the recognition and enforcement of the arbitral award. National arbitration laws, in addition, define the interaction between national courts and the arbitral tribunal and actually limit the extent of court intervention (see VII.). Many national arbitration laws are similar because over 80 states have used the Model Law as a basis for their national law on arbitration.

National arbitration laws usually do not cover details of the actual conduct of the arbitral proceedings. The national laws on civil procedure before state courts, however, do not apply to arbitral proceedings (unless the parties have explicitly agreed thereon, which is rarely done in practice). Therefore, there is no predetermined set of procedural rules which would apply to the arbitral proceedings. Rather, the parties are free to determine these rules and to tailor them to their needs depending on the particularities of the dispute. Quite often, the parties do not design a procedure specifically for their case. Instead – and rightly so – the parties agree on a set of procedural rules issued by arbitration institutions such as, for example, the ICC or national arbitration institutions like the Swedish SCC or the Austrian VIAC. The institutional rules are thus the second set of rules applicable to arbitral proceedings.

Third, the parties may agree on the application of guidelines or "rules" issued by organizations other than the arbitration institutions. The most renowned are the IBA Rules on the Taking of Evidence in International Arbitration. Strictly speaking, these "rules" only apply if the parties have agreed on their application. However, the IBA Rules frequently contain a kind of best practice standard. As a consequence, arbitral tribunals will often follow the IBA Rules, even in the absence of an express agreement by the parties to do so. Of course, this does not apply to the extent that the parties have agreed on something different.

Fourth, the recognition and enforcement of arbitral awards is, of course, equally governed by law. As set out above, the national arbitration laws determine under which conditions an award rendered in this state can be enforced in this state. When a party seeks to enforce an arbitral award rendered in a foreign state, the award has to be recognized and declared enforceable by the courts of the state in which enforcement is sought.

Finally, apart from the rules applicable to the arbitration as such, there is the law which is applicable to the substantial issues in dispute. The arbitrator(s) have to apply this law unless the parties have explicitly agreed otherwise. The parties may vest the arbitrator(s) with the power to decide "*ex aequo et bono*", i.e. guided by considerations of fairness and not a strict application of the law. Yet, this is very rare in practice.

The set of rules governing arbitral proceedings thus comprises:

- The national arbitration law (mandatory law at the seat of arbitration)
- Procedural rules for the actual conduct of the arbitral proceedings (chosen by the parties)
- Guidelines or "rules" issued by bar associations, most notably the IBA (chosen by the parties or applied as best practice standard)
- The law applicable to the substantial issues (e.g. the law governing the contract in dispute).

8. MEDIATION AND INTERNATIONAL ARBITRATION CAN BE INTERTWINED

It is relatively common, especially in contracts for large infrastructure or construction projects, to include a so-called multi-tier dispute resolution clause. This is a clause which provides for different stages of the dispute resolution process. The different stages involve separate procedures such as, for example, negotiation, mediation and finally arbitration. This can pose problems if it remains unclear under which conditions the next tier of the dispute resolution procedure can be utilized. It may also be unclear whether the completion of a tier, e.g. an attempt to mediate, is a precondition for the commencement of arbitration proceedings or not. The drafting of multi-tier clauses therefore involves some risks (for details see II. 7).

A multi-tier clause may already create a link between mediation and arbitration. Some clauses even reinforce this link by providing for so-called Med-Arb or Arb-Med proceedings. Med-Arb means that the parties have agreed to mediate their dispute first and, if mediation fails, to proceed to arbitration with the same person(s) acting both as mediator and arbitrator. Arb-Med means that the dispute resolution process begins with arbitral proceedings. These proceedings are interrupted at a certain point in time (usually just before the award is issued, which has already been drafted) and the arbitrator(s) conduct a mediation. If the mediation fails, the award is issued. It is also possible that the parties interrupt an ongoing arbitration at a certain point in time in order to conduct a mediation with a separate mediator. Arb-Med is rarely used in practice. Med-Arb is used more frequently, especially in Asian jurisdictions.

The Med-Arb procedure addresses a perceived disadvantage of "pure" mediation, namely the lack of a guarantee that the dispute will be finally resolved by an arbitral award if the mediation fails. In addition, Med-Arb has the advantage that an agreement reached can take the form of an arbitral award (on agreed terms). This is important if one party fears that it may have to enforce the agreement abroad. Due to the New York Convention, arbitral awards are usually easier to enforce than mere agreements. Furthermore, a combination of mediation and arbitration can lead to a more effective resolution of the dispute. This is because some aspects of the dispute may be resolved through mediation so that the subsequent arbitration proceedings can be limited to the remaining aspects. Even if the mediation fails completely, the time and money spent were not in vain. The effort to present the case in arbitration proceedings before the same person(s) is less than in completely separate arbitration proceedings. Finally, the parties may benefit from the use of mediation techniques during the arbitration phase.

However, such "hybrid" procedures raise, inter alia, the following problems:

- Will the parties put their cards on the table in the mediation when they know that the same person(s) will possibly decide the matter as arbitrator(s)? Probably not. This means that one of the main advantages of mediation is lost, namely that the parties disclose their interests in order to pave the way for an agreement which is not entirely rights-based.
- Can the information obtained during mediation be used in subsequent arbitration proceedings?
- Is the arbitral tribunal still independent and impartial if the same person has spoken to one side during mediation without the involvement of the other side (= caucus; see I. 3)? Therefore, the parties are well advised to carefully consider whether they really want a multi-tier approach involving the same persons at different stages of the proceedings.

Some institutions offer a set of rules also for hybrid proceedings, e.g. the Singapore International Mediation Centre (SIMC) with its SIAC-SIMC-Arb-Med-Arb Protocol.

9. MONEY LAUNDERING, BRIBERY AND CORRUPTION CASES POSE ETHICAL CHALLENGES IN ARBITRATION

Arbitral proceedings can be misused for money laundering purposes. This is because they may be used to legitimate a payment. How does it work? One party raises a spurious or inflated claim against an accomplice party. The respondent – on purpose – loses the case. The respondent complies with the arbitral award and makes a payment to the prevailing party, either in cash or even using the proceeds of a crime. The recipient can easily explain this payment by referring to the arbitral award.

Both arbitrators and lawyers should be alert to this possibility, as even passive assistance to money launderers is criminalized in many jurisdictions. There may also be reporting requirements. Apart from this, the prevention of money laundering is at least an ethical obligation.

Another ethical challenge are cases involving bribery or corruption. Generally speaking, arbitral tribunals have jurisdiction to hear cases involving such criminal behavior. It has occasionally been argued that an arbitral tribunal must decline jurisdiction because a contract tainted by corruption is null and void, and the parties to such a contract cannot validly ask for the assistance of an arbitral tribunal. However, according to the almost universally accepted doctrine of separability, the possible nullity of the contract does not affect the arbitration clause contained therein (see II. 9). Therefore, unless the arbitration agreement itself is a sham which cannot survive independently of the contract, the arbitral tribunal has jurisdiction to hear the case.

Whether the corrupt contract is valid or not is a different question. One has to distinguish between the main contract, which was concluded through corruption or bribery, and the third-party contract that provides for corruption or attempts to mask corruptive behavior (e.g. a "consultancy" or "agency" agreement). Under most laws, such third-party contracts are void *ab initio*. As regards the main contract, the situation is not that clear. Under some national laws, this contract is also null and void. Other laws stipulate that the contract is voidable. Finally, there are also laws under which the main contract is binding and enforceable. Apart from that, the definition of corruption varies in the different national laws.

Therefore, the determination of the applicable substantive law can have a decisive impact on the outcome of the arbitration. If the parties have not chosen the applicable law (which is relatively rare in practice) the arbitral tribunal has to decide on this issue. Arbitral tribunals have applied a wide range of solutions, including the application of various choice of law rules as well as the direct choice of the applicable law (e. g. the law at the seat of the arbitration or the law of the state in which the contract was performed). To further complicate the situation, arbitral tribunals have sometimes sought ways to circumvent the result which would follow from the evaluation of the contract under the governing law. Finally, corruption was often found to contravene transnational public policy. If this is determined, the corrupt act might invalidate the contract, even if this would not be the case under the applicable substantive law. However, this usually only applies to the illicit third-party contract, not to the main contract.

As a matter of principle, the burden of proof rests with the party asserting corruption. Most tribunals apply a high standard of proof (while the reasoning on which standard applies varies considerably). In addition, the parties usually seek to hide corrupt behavior, and the arbitral tribunal has little means to compel the production of evidence. As a consequence, a positive finding of corruption is very difficult to establish in practice. Thus, in most cases involving assertions of corruption, the arbitral tribunal has found that corruption has not been proven. Apart from that, arbitral tribunals have ruled on corruption on relatively few occasions. It appears that in some instances allegations of corruption are avoided by the tribunal or the parties. From an ethical point of view, however, it is desirable that arbitral tribunals do not shy away from making findings on corruption. The evidentiary barriers could be overcome, for example, by shifting the burden of proof under certain conditions or by drawing adverse inferences. The standard of proof could also be lowered and/or the tribunal could rely to a greater extent on circumstantial evidence.

10. INTERNATIONAL ARBITRATION OFFERS SIGNIFICANT ADVANTAGES

In some cases, international arbitration is without a real alternative. This proves true if the competent state courts are located in a country where the judiciary is not independent or where there is no developed legal system fulfilling basic standards of fairness (*cf.* X. 1). It is also a huge advantage that the parties can choose the arbitrators and select the persons they consider most suitable for resolving their dispute (see III. 4). In addition, the parties may find it preferable that arbitral proceedings are private, contrary to state court proceedings which are usually open to the public (see IV. 10). Last but not least, it is usually easier to enforce an arbitral award in a foreign country than a decision of a state court (see VIII. 1). This is mainly the case when the dispute is related to a country that is not a member of the European Union.

Nevertheless, some in-house counsels complain about international arbitration. Their primary complaint is inefficiency. This is mainly due to the fact that arbitration proceedings can take longer than state court proceedings and can be more expensive (for details see IX. 1). At first sight, this seems surprising. There are hardly any waiting times before arbitration proceedings begin, and – provided that the arbitrators are available (*cf.* III. 4) – the proceedings could be conducted much more quickly than before sometimes overloaded state courts. Moreover, arbitration proceedings are completed in one instance with no second instance review of the merits (*cf.* VIII. 8). However, the duration of arbitration proceedings depends on the self-discipline of the parties and the tribunal as well as on the adopted style of the arbitration: The common "Americanization" of international arbitration, which involves cross-examination by counsel and extensive document disclosure, leads to longer proceedings (see IV. 7).

Long proceedings result in high costs. Already the arbitrators' fees and the fees of the arbitral institution will often be higher than the court costs in state court proceedings (*cf.* II. 5). However, by far the largest part of the costs incurred in arbitration proceedings are the costs of the parties (see IX. 1) which increase with the duration of the proceedings. The parties therefore have the option to significantly reduce costs by working towards an efficient procedure. This is another advantage of arbitration – the parties are free to tailor the proceedings to their needs and to the specifics of the case. It is not advisable for the parties to write an entire procedural code for their proceedings (see III. 8). However, it is possible that the parties have a say in determining, for example, the number of briefs and the deadlines for their submission. The parties also benefit from the possibility to choose the extent to which they want to have document disclosure (see V. 2) and how witness examination is to be conducted (*cf.* IX. 1).

Many arbitral institutions have seen the problem of perceived inefficiency and have addressed it when revising their institutional rules. The German Arbitration Institute (DIS), for example, has shortened deadlines and introduced a mandatory early case management conference to discuss how to ensure procedural efficiency (Article 27 of the DIS Rules). In addition, many updated rules provide expedited procedure rules. The ICC, for example, has introduced the Expedited Procedure Provisions for small claims, i. e. claims where the amount in dispute does not exceed USD 3,000,000 (USD 2,000,000 if the arbitration agreement was concluded on or after 1 March 2017 and before 1 January 2021) (Article 30 of the ICC Rules and Appendix VI). The parties are also free to agree on the Expedited Procedure Provisions if the amount in dispute is higher (Article 30 (2) of the ICC Rules). Apart from that, Appendix IV of the ICC Rules sets out examples of case management techniques that can be used by the arbitral tribunal and the parties to control time and costs.

Finally, besides the choice of the institutional rules, the choice of the arbitrators and also of the seat of arbitration plays a significant role in the actual conduct of the arbitration proceedings. Arbitration proceedings seated in a civil law country with arbitrators from a civil law background will most likely be less "Americanized". The parties could go even further and agree with the arbitrators that they conduct the proceedings in the inquisitorial way that is commonly used by state court judges in civil law countries.

II.

THE ARBITRATION AGREEMENT

1. NO ARBITRATION WITHOUT CONSENT TO ARBITRATE

A party wishing to initiate arbitral proceedings must be able to establish that, at one point in time, the parties have agreed to have their dispute resolved by arbitration. The agreement to arbitrate is the door to any arbitration. It documents the parties' consent to submit potential disputes exclusively to arbitration. Consequently, claims brought before a national court are generally inadmissible.

There are two types of arbitration agreements: an arbitration clause as part of the contract between the parties about the underlying transaction, and the submission agreement. An arbitration clause is usually concluded long before a dispute arises, whereas a submission agreement is formed when the dispute has already arisen. The former and most common, is already contained in the principal agreement between the parties and is an agreement to submit future disputes to arbitration. The latter is an agreement to submit existing disputes to arbitration.

Arbitration clauses are usually short, and submission agreements are often long. This is not because of any particular legal requirement; it is simply a reflection of the situation. An arbitration clause dealing with disputes that may arise in the future usually does not go into too much detail, because the parties do not know what kind of dispute will arise and how it should best be handled. Indeed, although the parties to a contract may agree to an arbitration clause, they still hope that there will never be a dispute. Usually, in their principal agreement, the parties refer to a short model clause recommended by one of the arbitration institutions. Such arbitration clauses are described in more detail in II. 4.

By contrast, a submission agreement deals with a dispute that has already arisen, and therefore, the parties try to find a tailor-made solution for the particular case at hand. A submission agreement should contain all the basic elements of an arbitration agreement. In addition, it should contain a definition, or at least an outline, of the dispute to be arbitrated. It may also be advantageous to include further procedural arrangements, such as the procedural timetable to be followed, provisions for document production, the exchange of written submissions and witness or expert statements. The typical challenge in negotiating a submission agreement is that at this stage, there is already a hostile element in the relationship between the parties, and their interests differ quite substantially even with regard to procedural questions. The claimant usually wants to speed up the proceedings, whereas the respondent may want to take advantage of any possible delay. For all these reasons, the negotiation of a submission agreement can be a lengthy process.

Any agreement to arbitrate, be it an arbitration clause or a submission agreement, should be in line with some general principles and contain specific elements. According to Article 7 (2) of the Model Law, an arbitration agreement must be in writing. National arbitration laws may define the written form requirement of the arbitration agreement in greater detail (compare also Article 7 (3) to (5) of the Model Law). Under German law, for example, an arbitration agreement must normally be contained either in a document signed by the parties or in an exchange of letters, telefaxes, telegrams or other means of telecommunication recording the agreement (Section 1031 (1) of the German Code of Civil Procedure). If at least one party to the arbitration agreement is a consumer, Section 1031 (5) of the German Code of Civil Procedure provides that the arbitration agreement must be contained in a separate document signed by the parties.

In any case, the arbitration agreement must record the parties' intention to exclude the jurisdiction of the national courts and to refer a dispute to a private method of dispute resolution – namely arbitration. However, there are other important elements of an arbitration agreement:

1. The parties must determine which disputes they wish to finally resolve by arbitration. If the parties want to resort to institutional arbitration, they must indicate the selected institution or the rules of an institution which are to govern the conduct of the arbitration.
2. The seat of arbitration (sometimes also referred to as place of arbitration) is one of the most important matters to specify when drafting an arbitration agreement. This is because the national arbitration law of the seat governs the arbitral proceedings (for details see IV. 8).
3. The parties may want to agree on the language of proceedings, but if the language is not specified in the arbitration agreement, the arbitral tribunal will determine it.
4. Usually, an arbitration is heard by one or three arbitrators. An even number of arbitrators should always be avoided. Although cheaper, the choice of a sole arbitrator can be riskier as the award depends on the opinion of only one person.

2. OBJECTIVE ARBITRABILITY – NOT EVERY KIND OF DISPUTE CAN BE SUBMITTED TO ARBITRATION

The dispute referred to an arbitral tribunal must be "arbitrable". As each state can decide which disputes it wishes to reserve for resolution by state courts, arbitration is not necessarily admissible in every case. The "objective arbitrability" is also referred to as arbitrability *ratione materiae*. The latter term better describes that arbitrability here is about the subject matter in contrast to the parties to the dispute. In Germany, for example, all disputes involving an economic interest are in general arbitrable. Some disputes are, however, excluded from arbitration, such as certain disputes concerning the existence of domestic residential lease agreements or disputes concerning matters of employment law, criminal law, family law and law of succession.

The non-arbitrability doctrine raises complex choice-of-law questions in determining what law(s) apply to stipulate whether a claim or dispute is non-arbitrable. Part of the difficulty results from the fact that arbitrability questions can arise at different stages of the arbitral process triggering different choice-of-law considerations. The question of arbitrability can arise twofold: (a) either as an interlocutory matter, in which case it must be dealt with by the arbitral tribunal or by the courts at the seat of arbitration before the dispute can go to its merits; (b) or at the enforcement stage, where the question of arbitrability may arise even if the dispute has been deemed arbitrable at the seat of arbitration.

In principle, several choices of law to govern non-arbitrability questions are available: (a) the law of the state in which an arbitration agreement is sought to be enforced; (b) the law governing the parties' arbitration agreement; (c) the law of the seat of arbitration; (d) the law that provides the basis for the relevant substantive claim; (e) the law of the state in which the award is (potentially) enforced.

The practice of international arbitration proves that the issue of which law governs arbitrability is not an easy one and that the answer to this question may depend on the tribunal or court before which it is raised. In other words, the solution to the issue may vary depending on whether it is decided by an arbitral tribunal, by the state court to which one of the parties has concurrently submitted the dispute, or whether it is decided in the course of a setting-aside or enforcement procedure.

According to Article V (2) lit. a of the New York Convention, an award must not be recognized in a particular member state if "*[t]he subject matter of the difference is not capable of settlement by arbitration under the law of that country*". Article V (2) lit. a of the New York Convention simply stipulates that, at the time of enforcement of an award, a state may apply its own law to refuse recognition and enforcement of an otherwise valid and binding award on the grounds of non-arbitrability. Yet, in deviation from the clear wording, tribunals and courts have so far applied many different laws for the determination of objective arbitrability. Since tribunals, unlike state courts, are not the organs of a particular legal order such as state courts, in most cases they will apply the requirements of genuinely international public policy. Although some commentators have suggested so, it is generally accepted that Article V (2) lit. a of the New York Convention cannot be applied "by analogy" at the earlier stage of enforcing an arbitration agreement.

Irrespective of which law is to be applied, there are constellations in which questions of arbitrability are likely to arise, for example, when intellectual property, antitrust or insolvency issues are concerned. These constellations have in common that public rights and concerns are involved so that a resolution through state courts may be more appropriate. While some disputes concerning intellectual property rights can easily be referred to arbitration, the validity and grant of patents or trademarks are subject to the monopoly of state courts. Therefore, the latter acts are often considered not arbitrable. With respect to antitrust issues, it is nowadays widely accepted that antitrust issues concerning the validity of a contract are arbitrable. The arbitrability of insolvency issues is evaluated differently in different states. In any case, pure insolvency issues such as the adjudication of the insolvency itself, the collection and distribution of assets and the reorganization of a business are subject to state courts only.

The Model Law expressly states that this "*Law shall not affect any other law of this State by virtue of which certain disputes may not be submitted to arbitration or may be submitted to arbitration only according to provisions other than those of this Law*" (Article 1 (5) of the Model Law). It is therefore for each state to determine which matters may not be submitted to arbitration. Under German law, the relevant provision is Section 1030 (1) of the German Code of Civil Procedure which provides that any dispute of financial interest („*vermögensrechtlicher Anspruch*") may be the subject of an arbitration. In addition, disputes without financial interest are also arbitrable as long as the parties are able to conclude an agreement on this. The term financial interest has to be interpreted in a very broad sense including also declaratory claims as well as claims for injunctive relief. Arbitrability has to be denied for claims which are reserved for state courts by provisions grounded by public policy concerns. Such claims are, for example, claims based on a residential rental agreement or claims in non-pecuniary family law matters.

If the arbitral tribunal finds that the subject matter is non-arbitrable under the applicable law, the tribunal must decline to accept jurisdiction *ex officio*, even if the parties do not raise the issue during the proceedings.

3. IN DUBIO PRO ARBITRARE? – CONSENT IS A GREY AREA

Arbitration agreements can suffer from many different defects. The most frequent are inconsistency, uncertainty, and inoperability. In this respect, the term "pathological arbitration clause" is often used. If any such defect occurs, the question arises whether the defect has any impact on the validity of the arbitration agreement.

One of the most common errors is the reference to a non-existing arbitration institution. This error is negligible if the real intention of the parties can still be identified. The ICC Rules explicitly provide only for a *prima facie* examination of the arbitration agreement. Article 6 (4) of the ICC Rules states as follows: "*[…] The arbitration shall proceed if and to the extent that the Court is prima facie satisfied that an arbitration agreement under the Rules may exist. […]*". The ICC has in the past accepted the following vague and imprecise formulations as references to ICC arbitration: "the official Chamber of Commerce in Paris, France", "the Arbitration Commission of the Chamber of Commerce and Industry of Paris", and "a Commission of Arbitration of the French Chamber of Commerce, Paris". The ICC has even accepted clauses referring to the International Chamber of Commerce in connection with a specific place other than Paris or France. Such clauses are interpreted in favor of the ICC, while the place named by the parties is interpreted as the seat of arbitration.

If a claimant submits a claim that is based on an ambiguous arbitration clause, also most other institutions will only refuse to administer the case in extreme cases. As tribunals have a preliminary competence to decide on their own jurisdiction (the so-called competence-competence), the institutions leave it to the tribunal to decide. However, the tribunal's decision on its own jurisdiction is always subject to the control of the state courts at the seat of arbitration. Theoretically, in a worst case scenario, neither an arbitral tribunal nor a state court might decide to handle the case, because the tribunal considers the arbitration clause invalid and refers the parties to domestic courts, while the latter consider the clause valid and refer the dispute to arbitration.

Fortunately, this scenario is very unlikely, because with respect to inconsistencies and uncertainties, most national courts are generally inclined to uphold arbitration provisions unless the uncertainty is such that it is impossible to find a meaningful interpretation. Courts take this pro-arbitration approach if the agreement is a manifestation of the parties' intention to arbitrate. If the fundamental intention to exclude state jurisdiction is given, any uncertainties, errors and inconsistencies will usually be forgiven in order to give effect to the party agreement. This is different if the ambiguity relates to the mandatory element of an arbitration agreement, namely the binding submission of the dispute to a private arbitral tribunal. If such an intention is not identifiable, courts will usually be reluctant to apply an arbitration-friendly approach.

In England, for instance, the courts simply strike out the inconsistent provision if it is clear that the remaining clause reflects the real intention of the parties and the "discarded clause" would defeat the object of the agreement. The same approach has been adopted by U.S. courts with respect to non-existent arbitration fora. They usually tend to interpret such a clause as an agreement on arbitration without any institutional framework.

The Singapore courts upheld an agreement that referred disputes to "the Arbitration Committee at Singapore under the rules of the International Chamber of Commerce".

A German court found that the reference to "the International Court of Arbitration (Internationales Schiedsgericht) in Austria" was a reference to the international arbitration center of the Austrian Federal Economic Chamber.

Still, there is a risk that defects may affect the validity of an agreement. Some courts have indeed invalidated arbitration agreements referring to non-existent arbitration institutions by arguing that the parties' agreement could not be fulfilled as stipulated in the agreement and that it is not the task of the court to rewrite the contract.

4. DON'T REINVENT THE WHEEL (OR DON'T DRAFT, JUST COPY)

As mentioned before, most commercial arbitrations take place pursuant to an arbitration clause in a commercial contract. It is much less likely that parties submit their dispute to arbitration through a submission agreement after the dispute has already arisen.

There is a long list of commentaries on the drafting of arbitration agreements. In most cases, however, any advice on the drafting of an individual arbitration clause is superfluous, because a standard arbitration clause, recommended either by the arbitration institution to which the parties refer or by UNCITRAL for *ad hoc* proceedings, usually perfectly serves its purpose (for details on *ad hoc* proceedings see II. 5). Any subsequent arbitration will take place either according to the rules of the institution concerned or of UNCITRAL. These rules are generally adequate to guide the process from beginning to end without the need to include further regulations in the arbitration clause.

Experience in negotiating complex commercial contracts shows that dispute resolution clauses are often "midnight clauses". They are the last clauses to be considered in contract negotiations, sometimes late at night or early in the morning. In addition, the parties are often reluctant to consider the scenario of a dispute and therefore spend only insufficient effort on the dispute resolution scheme.

Under most well developed jurisdictions, minimalist arbitration clauses such as "resolution of disputes: arbitration, Frankfurt/Main" would be considered a valid agreement to arbitrate. Nevertheless, it is recommendable to use a standard arbitration clause of one of the well-known arbitration institutions. A short description of the major institutions can be found under II. 6.

If parties wish to agree on arbitration under the rules of the German Arbitration Institute, for example, the recommended model clause reads as follows:

> "All disputes arising out of or in connection with this contract or its validity shall be finally settled in accordance with the Arbitration Rules of the German Arbitration Institute (DIS) without recourse to the ordinary courts of law."

Furthermore, the clause should specify the state in which the arbitration is to take place ("*The seat of arbitration is [Frankfurt am Main, Germany]*"). This is an important choice as the law applicable to arbitrations taking place in the particular state will apply (see IV. 8). Therefore, it is very important to choose a state that has a modern and arbitration-friendly law. In any event, it is highly recommendable to choose a state that is a member state of the New York Convention. This is to ensure that the award is also enforceable in other New York Convention signatory states.

In addition, it is recommendable to add some further regulations with respect to the number of arbitrators (usually three), the language of the arbitral proceedings and the applicable substantive law.

Sticking to the aforementioned recommendations avoids creating a so-called pathological arbitration clause, which would be void in the worst case, but would in any case cause delays and unnecessary disputes before the actual arbitration begins. Examples for such pathological clauses are:

1. institution referred to does not exist;
2. naming of specific arbitrator who is unable or unwilling to act;
3. definition of certain qualifications for the arbitrators which cannot be fulfilled;
4. inconsistency in choice of seat of arbitration;
5. unrealistic deadline for the rendering of the award.

As mentioned before, parties who have chosen a particular institution to administer their arbitration are well advised to adopt this institution's model clause to mitigate the risks of a jurisdictional fight. Nonetheless, model clauses are not perfect for each and every situation and should be tailored in certain situations, for example, where the remedies likely to be required are not for monetary compensation (e.g. in company law disputes) and where one party is a state-owned enterprise, a state or a consumer.

5. INSTITUTIONAL ARBITRATION IS PREFERABLE TO AD HOC ARBITRATION

Once the parties to a contract have agreed on arbitration as the dispute resolution mechanism, the question often arises as to whether they should refer to the rules of a specific arbitration institution (institutional arbitration) or simply leave it with the agreement to arbitrate (*ad hoc* arbitration). The latter means that the arbitration is not administered by an institution.

Referring to the rules of a well-known arbitration institution and consequently agreeing on institutional arbitration is generally preferable. The most important advantage of institutional arbitration is that due to pre-established rules and procedures, it is usually ensured that the arbitral proceedings begin in a timely manner and with administrative assistance from the institution. If necessary, the institution can also assist the parties in nominating a qualified arbitrator. For this purpose, most institutions have a list of potential arbitrators available. An institution's panel of arbitrators usually consists of experts from different regions of the world. This allows the parties to select an arbitrator possessing the necessary skills, experience and expertise to provide for a quick and effective dispute resolution process. Although the parties nominate "their" arbitrator (usually each party one of the three arbitrators, while the chairperson is nominated by the party-nominated arbitrators), it is the institution's decision to actually appoint the tribunal. This is another advantage, since the institution regularly acts as the decision-making body in a potential dispute about the impartiality of one of the arbitrators. A further benefit of institutional arbitration is that the parties and arbitrators can seek assistance and advice from the institutional staff.

In general, arbitration can only be an option as a dispute resolution mechanism if it provides a final and binding award in the end. However, there is the inherent risk that a mistake made by a tribunal cannot be rectified at a later stage. In order to counterbalance this risk to some extent, some institutional rules (for example Article 34 of the ICC Rules) provide for a scrutiny of the draft award before the final award is issued. However, this is not intended to be a full second review of the merits of the case. Rather, the institution ensures that the award is adequately reasoned and deals with all issues of the proceeding, including interest and costs.

As always in life, where there is light, there is also shadow. The main disadvantages of institutional arbitration are the administrative fees for the services of the institution. These fees are usually higher than state court fees. The following example gives a good impression: In Germany, for an amount in dispute of EUR 10 million, state court fees come to about EUR 125,000, whereas fees for arbitration under the rules of the German Arbitration Institute ("DIS") amount to approx. EUR 240,000. Under the ICC Rules, the fees would even amount to roughly EUR 350,000.

Conversely, an *ad hoc* arbitration is not administered by an institution (such as ICC, LCIA, DIS, SCC, etc.). Therefore, the parties have to determine all aspects of the arbitration themselves, without any support by an institution. Provided that the parties follow a cooperative approach, *ad hoc* proceedings have the potential to be more flexible, faster and cheaper than institutional proceedings. The arbitration agreement, whether formulated in the principal agreement as an arbitration clause or as a submission agreement after a dispute has arisen, can simply state that "disputes between the parties will be arbitrated". Furthermore, it is recommendable to specify at least the seat of arbitration because this will determine the procedural laws governing the arbitration and the enforceability of the award (see IV. 8). Should one party refuse to comply with the agreement to arbitrate, the state courts at the seat of arbitration are competent to decide this issues.

A properly structured *ad hoc* arbitration is likely to be more cost-effective because the parties will only have to pay fees for the arbitrators, lawyers or representatives and the costs of conducting the proceedings, rather than paying fees to an arbitral institution. The parties negotiate the arbitrators' fees directly with the arbitrators, which leaves room for price negotiations, whereas in institutional arbitration the arbitrators' fees are determined by the institution. Conducting an *ad hoc* arbitration does not necessarily mean that the parties may not refer to any pre-established rules. The parties to a contract could refer to the rules of an institution or to the UNCITRAL Arbitration Rules, which are tailored to *ad hoc* arbitrations. Referring to the rules of an arbitration institution instead carries risks. For example, almost all rules drawn up by institutional providers refer to specific administration services rendered by the provider – such as appointmenting the members of the tribunal. These rules would have to be amended or excluded. This bears the risk of creating ambiguities or that the parties unintentionally create an institutional process.

However, another important disadvantage of *ad hoc* arbitration is that its effectiveness depends on how willing the parties are to agree on the arbitration procedures at a time when there may already be a dispute. The failure of one or both parties to fully cooperate can ultimately result in a time-consuming recourse to state court, e. g. if the parties cannot agree on the appointment of arbitrators or if an arbitrator is to be replaced because he is biased or delays the proceedings.

6. CHOOSING A GOOD ARBITRATION INSTITUTION IS IMPORTANT

The previous chapter explained why institutional arbitration is usually preferable to *ad hoc* arbitration. But the decision to conduct administered arbitral proceedings is only the first step. The next step is to choose the right arbitration institution. In view of the very large number of different arbitration institutions, there are a few aspects to consider when making the decision. There are regional, domestic and international institutions. In addition, one can differentiate between institutions that serve a particular trade or industry and other institutions that do not. Most institutions have one thing in common: an individual set of rules and an individual model clause which should be adopted and incorporated into the agreement (see II. 4).

First of all, it is important that the rules of the institution are constantly reviewed and, if necessary, revised and adapted to new developments in international arbitration, since international arbitration is a rapidly changing and developing practice.

Second, different arbitration institutions have different approaches to costs, which can be an important factor when choosing the institution. Some institutions determine their fees and the arbitrators' fees on the basis of amounts in dispute. Others calculate the fees on the basis of the time spent on the case. It is not possible to say whether one of these approaches is generally more favorable, since it always depends on the complexity of the case and the amount in dispute.

Third, it is important that the institution has highly qualified administrative staff, which is responsible for supporting the arbitral tribunal as well as for administrative tasks. In this respect, it is of utmost importance that the institution is able to administer the proceedings in the determined language.

In most cases, parties turn to one of the few established international arbitration institutions. These institutions are experienced, highly skilled and have proven that they administer and supervise the proceedings very well and almost everywhere in the world. Therefore, leading and established arbitration institutions are more predictable and better assessable than unknown or recently founded institutions. The world's leading and best-known arbitration institution is the International Chamber of Commerce's ("ICC") International Court of Arbitration in Paris, which was established in 1923. The ICC permanently administers a very large number of cases, most of which are international disputes involving parties from all over the world. The ICC provides for a highly qualified, multilingual secretariat, which is under the supervision of the ICC Court of Arbitration. The ICC Court is the administrative body for ICC arbitrations. Two special features of ICC arbitration are, firstly, the requirement for terms of reference to be drawn up at the outset of the proceedings, and, secondly, the ICC Court's scrutiny of the draft awards. The ICC, which published its revised set of rules in 2021 after the last changes were implemented in 2017, is a perfect example of up-to-dateness.

A very popular Continental European arbitration institution is the Deutsche Institution für Schiedsgerichtsbarkeit e. V. ("DIS") (German Arbitration Institute), which was formed in 1992 by the merger of Deutscher Ausschuss für Schiedsgerichtsbarkeit (German Association of Arbitration) and Deutsches Institut für Schiedsgerichtsbarkeit (German Institute of Arbitration). The DIS Arbitration Rules, in their most recent version effective since March 2018, are available for the resolution of disputes both on a national and international level.

Also worth mentioning is the London Court of International Arbitration ("LCIA"), which was founded in 1892. The LCIA has a relatively small group of administrative staff compared to the ICC, for instance, but its rules are more detailed than those of the ICC. It has a significant international caseload, including cases from Russia and countries of the former Russian confederation.

The American Arbitration Association ("AAA"), which administers a considerable number of "domestic" arbitrations within the United States of America, also administers interstate arbitrations. In order to cope with the increasing number of such arbitrations, the AAA established the International Center for Dispute Resolution ("ICDR") with several offices around the world.

International arbitration institutions have also come to the fore in Asia. The China International Economic and Trade Arbitration Center ("CIETAC") was established in Beijing in 1956 and has a regional arbitration center in Hong Kong, which was established in 1985. The current CIETAC Arbitration Rules, which came into force in January 2015, constitute a modern set of rules that is consistent with the internationalization of Chinese arbitration practice and procedure.

In 1991, the SIAC was founded in Singapore to provide a dispute resolution center for Asia. Singapore's law on arbitration is based on the Model Law, and the SIAC maintains a list of experienced arbitrators from all parts of the world from which the parties can choose their arbitrator if they so wish. The revised SIAC Arbitration Rules, which came into effect in August 2016, constitute a complete, modern set of rules.

Of course, the list of the aforementioned institutions is not conclusive, and there are many more that could be referred to (such as the Swiss Chambers' Arbitration Institution ("SCAI") with its "Swiss Rules", the Arbitration Institute of the Stockholm Chamber of Commerce with its "SCC Rules"), the Hong Kong International Arbitration Centre with its "HKIAC Rules", or the Vienna International Arbitral Centre (VIAC) with its "Vienna Rules"). In the end, users have to decide which features of an arbitration are most important to them and accordingly choose the arbitration institution.

7. MULTI-TIER CLAUSES – ARBITRATION MIGHT ONLY BE THE LAST RESORT

Multi-tier clauses are contract clauses that provide for at least two consecutive stages of dispute resolution mechanisms for disputes arising out of or in connection with the respective contract. Such clauses are also called escalation clauses or step clauses. By incorporating such clauses in an agreement, the parties intend to conduct arbitral proceedings as a last resort. The parties agree that before submitting the dispute to an arbitral tribunal, they must first try to find an amicable solution, *i. e.* to de-escalate the dispute. The parties are free to choose the procedures. Multi-tier clauses can include waiting periods, negotiations between corporate representatives, conciliation, mediation, or mini-trials. Some multi-tier clauses even include a referral to an expert or a third party for a non-binding opinion. In most multi-tier clauses, the parties agree to first attempt to resolve their dispute by negotiation (sometimes with escalation to more senior corporate representatives), followed by mediation, with arbitration only being permitted after these non-binding means of dispute resolution have failed.

Multi-tier clauses can contribute significantly to the time and cost efficiency of the dispute resolution process. If the amicable resolution is successful, the parties will not have to go through the more time-consuming and expensive process of arbitration. Needless to say that, on the other hand, multi-tier clauses can also have a delaying effect if the settlement negotiations fail.

The main question is whether or not multi-tier clauses and the commitment to finding an amicable solution in the first place are binding and enforceable. This is also essential for the question of whether or not the parties can be in breach of the agreement if they either fail to find an amicable solution or if they initiate arbitration proceedings despite the multi-tier agreement. In this regard, the wording of the clause is decisive. Clauses like "The parties agree to negotiate before initiating arbitration proceedings" cause problems due to their vagueness and lack of certainty about the scope of the negotiations.

It would be very difficult for a court or tribunal to decide on the basis of such a vague wording on a breach of this multi-tier clause. Such a clause does not provide for objective criteria to decide whether the parties are in compliance or breach of the provision. Although there are some differences in the way national courts around the world deal with the question of whether multi-tier clauses are enforceable, it is highly recommendable to draft precise multi-tier agreements that provide for a procedural framework and time limits as well as the respective obligations of the parties.

In order to avoid any doubt as to whether a stage of dispute resolution has been "performed" as agreed, it is recommendable to define clear deadlines or notification requirements. In any case, is not advisable to include the requirement that the parties may only proceed to the next stage of the dispute resolution escalation by mutual agreement.

A well drafted multi-tier clause may read as follows:

> [First Tier] Any dispute arising out of or in connection with this contract shall be settled through negotiations between the parties.
>
> [Second Tier] If subsequent to a written notice of one party a dispute cannot be settled through negotiations as provided for in subsection 1 within four weeks or any longer period agreed upon by the parties, then either party must refer the dispute to mediation according to the Mediation Rules of the German Arbitration Institute (Deutsche Institution für Schiedsgerichtsbarkeit e. V., "DIS").
>
> [Third Tier] If the mediator notifies both parties or one party notifies the other party in writing that the mediation initiated pursuant to subsection 2 has failed, each party may refer the dispute to arbitration according to the Rules of Arbitration of the German Arbitration Institute. The dispute shall be decided by three arbitrators. The seat of arbitration shall be [...]. The language of the arbitration shall be [...].

8. COMPLEX TRANSACTIONS REQUIRE COMPLEX PRECAUTIONS – MULTI-CONTRACT AND MULTI-PARTY SITUATIONS

Not every commercial transaction or contract is executed by just two parties. There may be one contract but more than two parties ("multi-party"), a number of contracts between the same parties ("multi-contract"), or a number of contracts with different parties (multi-party, multi-contract). The parties' consent is the fundamental keystone of international arbitration and is therefore always required for the conduct of arbitral proceedings. It is embodied in the arbitration agreement between the parties, which determines the tribunal's jurisdiction and powers.

As a consequence of the consensual element of international arbitration, an arbitration agreement only binds the parties to the agreement, but not others. This is the basic rule. However, there are cases where the arbitration agreement might also bind (and benefit) third parties.

There are various ways to achieve such third-party effects: first, by operation of the "group of companies" doctrine; second, by operation of general rules of private law (e.g. succession); or third, by way of joinder or intervention under certain circumstances.

The group of companies doctrine states that the benefits and duties arising from an arbitration agreement may, under certain circumstances, be extended to other members of the same group of companies. The Dow Chemical case has been invoked as the leading authority on the group of companies doctrine. In this case, a claim was successfully brought before an ICC tribunal not only by the companies that had signed the relevant agreements, but also by their parent company, a US corporation, and a French subsidiary of the same group. However, there are also tribunals and courts that reject the group of companies doctrine. In the Netherlands, for example, an award binding non-signatory affiliates was annulled. Also Swiss and English courts have refused to accept that a third party be bound by an arbitration agreement merely because it has a commercial relationship with one of the parties. In light of the Dow Chemical case and the aforementioned court decisions, it is clear that there is only very limited scope for applying the group of companies doctrine. Only if (a) the non-signatory actively participated in the conclusion of the contract containing the arbitration agreement, and (b) the non-signatory has a clear interest in the outcome of the dispute, there is room for a tribunal to bind third parties to an arbitration agreement.

A third party may also be bound by an arbitration agreement by operation of general rules of private law, such as legal succession. For example, if two companies merge, the "surviving" company will be the legal successor that owns all the assets and liabilities (including contract rights and obligations) of the previously existing entities. The "surviving" company therefore succeeds by operation of law as a party to the contracts including the arbitration agreement.

Third parties can also become part of arbitral proceedings by way of joinder or intervention. Both joinder and intervention are only possible with the consent of all parties concerned. The parties to the arbitration agreement can explicitly or implicitly agree on a joinder or intervention or simply refer to the institutional arbitration rules which provide for them. Joinder refers to the situation in which, upon request of an existing ("original") party to an arbitration, a third party not yet involved in this arbitration is ordered to participate in the proceedings as claimant or respondent. By means of an intervention, a third party may, on its own initiative, request to participate in the arbitral proceedings between the parties to the arbitration agreement.

Joining arbitration proceedings as a third party may be problematic if the tribunal has already been constituted. It is important to ensure that all parties are treated equally and, if relevant, that the procedure for participation in the appointment of the tribunal is respected.

Most arbitration rules contain a provision with respect to the joinder of third parties. For example, Article 7 (1) of the ICC Rules permits a party to file a "Request for Joinder" against a third party (a) before the appointment of an arbitrator, if there is an arbitration agreement under the ICC Rules that binds all the parties, and (b) after the appointment of an arbitrator, if all the parties, including the third party, agree and if there is an arbitration agreement under the ICC Rules that binds all the parties.

Article 22.1 (viii) of the LCIA Rules permits the joinder of a third party upon the application of a party if the third party has declared its consent. There is no explicit requirement that the third party must be a party to the arbitration agreement, so this should permit joinder in multi-contract situations. In contrast, Article 7 of the SIAC Rules permits third parties to join an arbitration only if the third party is a party to the arbitration agreement and consents in writing to the joinder.

Most institutional rules do not provide for intervention (voluntary intervention in an existing arbitration by a third party). If parties wish to allow intervention, they should include bespoke provision to that effect in the arbitration agreement. In the absence of such regulation, intervention is only possible if all parties declare their consent.

9. TERMINATING A CONTRACT LEAVES THE ARBITRATION CLAUSE UNAFFECTED

Like other issues of validity, questions of termination of the arbitration agreement must be considered in connection with the so-called separability presumption. This means that even if the tribunal considers the principle agreement that includes the arbitration clause to be invalid, it still has the authority to confirm or reject its competence to decide the dispute under the invalid contract. Article 16 (1) of the Model Law mentions this principle in clear words and provides that

> "an arbitration clause which forms part of a contract shall be treated as an agreement independent of the other terms of the contract. The decision by the arbitral tribunal that the contract is null and void shall not entail ipso iure the invalidity of the arbitration clause".

The principle of separability is also set out in Section 1040 (1) of the German Code of Civil Procedure.

In most jurisdictions, national courts have held that the termination of the principle contract does not affect the parties' arbitration agreement. The judgment of a German appellate court provides a good quotation as to the consequences of the termination of the principle agreement:

> "[T]ermination of the agency contract does not mean that the arbitration clause therein also became null and void at the same time. The main contract and arbitration clause are strictly separable. The main contract is a substantive law agreement, whereas the arbitration clause is a procedural agreement."

Due to their procedural nature, arbitration agreements cannot be terminated unilaterally by one party. Rather, it is presumed that the arbitration agreement shall remain in force unless the parties agree otherwise. Any other result would allow parties to unilaterally abrogate their mutually agreed dispute resolution mechanism when a dispute arises, which commercially makes no sense. Moreover, a party cannot unilaterally terminate the arbitration agreement by submitting the dispute to national courts. Since arbitral tribunals have the preliminary competence to decide on their own jurisdiction, the court will rather refer the dispute to arbitration.

Although the termination of the underlying contract does not terminate the separable arbitration clause, it is nonetheless possible for the parties to terminate the arbitration agreement separately. In one court's words:

"There is nothing irrevocable about an agreement to arbitrate".

In most jurisdictions, an arbitration agreement may be terminated by mutual consent, just as other contracts may be terminated by mutual consent. In practice, however, commercial parties very rarely actually intend to terminate their arbitration agreement, but only the principle contract. In this way, the agreed-upon dispute resolution mechanism stays in place for all disputes that may emerge from their contract while it was in effect. Therefore, a termination of the principle contract will almost never be interpreted as a termination of the separable arbitration agreement, unless the parties express their actual intention to do so.

Under certain circumstances, a party may want to waive its right under an arbitration agreement to have a dispute finally settled by litigation. Under most national laws, such a waiver typically requires a statement or a conduct that amounts to renunciation of the right to arbitrate. Such conduct can be found in a party's participation in national court proceedings dealing with a subject matter that is covered by an arbitration agreement. Under German law, the respondent has to raise the arbitration agreement as a defense prior to the beginning of the oral hearing on the substance of the dispute. Consequently, the court must reject the claim as inadmissible if it deems the arbitration agreement valid.

10. ARBITRATION AGREEMENTS IN STANDARD TERMS MAY BE VOID OR SUBJECT TO SPECIFIC LEGAL REQUIREMENTS FOR VALIDITY

Arbitration agreements can generally be found as standard terms in two scenarios. First, a standard arbitration agreement may be included in the main document of an otherwise individually drafted contract. Second, it may be contained in a separate document. This separate document may (a) contain other standard terms, (b) be signed or not, and (c) be referred to in the main document. Furthermore, the reference can be made to the standard terms in general or to the standard arbitration clause in particular.

If an arbitration agreement is included in standard terms, the issue of consent may arise. The requirements for a valid consent can be particularly strict if a consumer is involved. In any case, there is not one single international solution to this issue, but the national law governing the arbitration agreement must be analyzed.

Although the arbitration agreement may be included in standard terms, the arbitration agreement is generally a separate contract and therefore underlies its own governing law. If no law governing the arbitration agreement has been chosen, the law at the seat of arbitration is relevant.

If German law applies, Sections 305 et seq. of the German Civil Code must generally be respected, even if no consumer is involved. These provisions prohibit in particular surprising clauses (Section 305c (1) of the German Civil Code). According to German case law, it is relevant whether arbitration clauses are common in the industry sector concerned. Albeit the academic discussion of this topic, there are rarely cases in which a court has found an arbitration clause to be surprising and thus void.

In addition, pursuant to Section 307 of the German Civil Code, the arbitration clause must ensure a fair trial. This rather broad statutory provision leaves room for some interpretation. Although there might be very few cases in which one party takes advantage of its economic power to establish an unjust regulation for an arbitration, arbitration clauses will not be considered to establish an unfair trial if the parties used a standard clause of one of the well-known institutions and did not make any amendments, for example regarding the nomination of arbitrators by only one party.

If both parties to a contract refer to their own standard terms, and these standard terms provide for different dispute resolution mechanisms, the question arises: which of the conflicting dispute resolution clauses is relevant? According to Article 7 (5) Option I of the Model Law, an arbitration agreement exists if the

> "existence of an agreement is alleged by one party and not denied by the other".

This rule can also be referred to as the "Last Shot Rule", because only the standard terms last referred to are incorporated. This rule is popular in common law countries but heavily criticized in civil law countries for disregarding the parties' true intentions.

For this reason, many civil law countries follow the so-called "Knock-out Rule" and not the "Last Shot Rule". According to the "Knock-out Rule", those clauses of each party's standard terms are incorporated that do not contradict the other party's standard terms. If clauses contradict the other party's terms, these clauses are not incorporated. German statutory law does not expressly provide for either one or the other rule. However, the German Federal Court of Justice argues that each party's clauses can only be incorporated to the extent that they correspond to the other party's clauses ("principle of congruent validity") and thus follows the "Knock-out Rule". This means that if one party's standard terms provide for an arbitration clause, arbitration is the binding dispute resolution mechanism only if the other party's standard terms do not provide for another dispute resolution mechanism, such as state court litigation or arbitration under different rules.

III.

THE ARBITRAL TRIBUNAL

1. DISPUTES MAY BE REFERRED TO SOLE ARBITRATORS OR TO TRIBUNALS

One of the most important advantages of arbitration over state court litigation is that parties can choose their judges, i. e. the arbitrators. Parties can choose not only who should be their arbitrator, but also how many arbitrators they want to have decide their dispute. The number of arbitrators matters for various reasons:

First, it makes a difference whether one person decides alone or if a group of individuals (= a tribunal) discusses and decides a case together. Every lawyer who has ever been to court knows that while a single judge might be quicker, a tribunal often makes more reasoned decisions. Three brains are (usually!) better than one. At the very least, the margin of error tends to be smaller.

Second, it is important to consider the group dynamics of arbitral tribunals. In each group, one person usually turns out to be the group leader defining the behavior (= decision) of the group. It is often difficult for other group members to assert themselves against the group leader. This is particularly true if one member of the group has (*i*) greater expertise on a certain topic than the others or (*ii*) a higher reputation in the respective field. In such cases, other group members tend to follow the views of this person because they believe he or she (probably) knows best, even if they would have decided otherwise individually. In an arbitral tribunal, this person should ideally be the tribunal's president.

Third, arbitration with a sole arbitrator is cheaper than arbitration with a tribunal consisting of three or more arbitrators. The parties only have to pay the fees and expenses of one arbitrator instead of three or more.

Theoretically, parties can choose any number of arbitrators: two, seven, thirteen. Article 10 (1) of the Model Law explicitly states that the parties "*determine the number of arbitrators*", i. e. any number (*cf.* also Section 1034 (1) of the German Code of Civil Procedure). In practice, however, parties usually rely on either a sole arbitrator or a tribunal of three arbitrators to decide their dispute. This is also reflected in the Model Law as well as in the German arbitration law where it is stipulated as a default rule that in the absence of an agreement by the parties, a tribunal will consist of three arbitrators (*cf.* Article 10 (2) of the Model Law and Section 1034 (1) of the German Code of Civil Procedure; Article 10 of the DIS Rules). Some countries prohibit arbitration by an even number of arbitrators, e. g. Article 809 of the Italian Code of Civil Procedure, because of the possibility of a stalemate. Arbitration agreements stipulating an even number of arbitrators are dealt with inconsistently in such prohibiting countries: sometimes, the national laws alter the agreements to an odd number of arbitrators; in other countries, such arbitration agreements are considered invalid.

Often, parties mechanically prefer an arbitral tribunal over a sole arbitrator when drafting their arbitration agreement or starting proceedings. While in many cases it makes sense to have an arbitral tribunal, sometimes a sole arbitrator is the better choice. In-house counsel should therefore always consider the specific character of their dispute. In particular, they should be mindful of the time and cost efficiency of the dispute resolution process. For example, in-house counsel need to consider the following aspects of their dispute:

- history and complexity (factual and legal)
- number and nationalities of parties involved
- amount in dispute.

Disputes involving simple facts and where the amount in dispute is rather small can often be efficiently decided by a sole arbitrator. In contrast, in cases where the parties are from different countries and do not speak the same language, where a significant amount is in dispute or where the dispute revolves around complex (technical) issues, it probably makes sense to rely upon an arbitral tribunal. This is because in an arbitral tribunal, each party has the possibility of appointing an arbitrator who has the special skills required to resolve the dispute.

Of course, an arbitral tribunal consisting of three arbitrators is more expensive than a sole arbitrator. But not three times as expensive! Only the fee for the president of the tribunal is the same as the fee for the sole arbitrator. Under most arbitration rules, the fees for the president and the co-arbitrators differ. For example, under the DIS Rules, a co-arbitrator's fee is 30 % lower than the president's fee (*cf.* § 2.1 of Annex 2 of the DIS Rules). The difference can even be up to 40 % (Article 2 (1) of Appendix IV of the SCC Rules). However, one important exception are the ICC Rules. The ICC Court fixes the costs of the arbitration which include the fees of all arbitrators (Article 38 (1) of the ICC Rules). It is then up to the arbitrators how they divide the fees among themselves. Most of the time, the president of a panel of three arbitrators receives 40 % of the total fee, while each co-arbitrator receives 30 %. The parties must also not forget the arbitrators' expenses, which are generally reimbursed by the parties (e. g. travel expenses). In this regard, three arbitrators are three times more expensive than a sole arbitrator.

2. THE END DOES NOT JUSTIFY THE MEANS (OR THE IMPORTANCE OF FOLLOWING THE APPOINTMENT PROCEDURE)

In general, arbitrators are chosen by the parties. The principle of party autonomy is a cornerstone of arbitration, in particular when it comes to the appointment procedure. The selection of an arbitrator is probably the most important decision to be made in an arbitration. If the parties have agreed on an arbitral tribunal with three arbitrators, the two co-arbitrators are appointed in the following three steps: (*i*) selection, (*ii*) nomination, and (*iii*) confirmation.

First, each party selects its own arbitrator. The importance of selecting the "right" or "best" arbitrator for a specific case cannot be overstated. Choosing an unfit arbitrator deprives a party of one of the advantages of arbitration, namely the possibility to have an expert decide the case. It is not uncommon that parties later regret their selection if they have not chosen wisely.

Second, the party then formally nominates its arbitrator. Usually, the claimant goes first and is then followed by the respondent. The nomination must be sent to the arbitration institution and is often part of the request for arbitration or the answer.

Third, the institution confirms the arbitrator. Before doing so, the institution asks the arbitrator to accept the nomination and to provide a declaration of independence and impartiality (Article 9 of the DIS Rules; Article 13 (2) of the ICC Rules). This declaration is important as it can give the other party grounds to challenge the arbitrator (see III. 6).

Once both co-arbitrators are confirmed, the same three-step procedure is repeated for the nomination of the president of the tribunal. However, there is one difference: Not the parties, but the co-arbitrators select and nominate the president. However, it is not uncommon that each co-arbitrator consults with the party that nominated him or her about possible candidates. Legally, this is not a problem – even though all arbitrators must be independent and impartial – as long as the co-arbitrators are free to decide on the nomination of the president in the end. Such consultation is part of each party's ability to choose its arbitrators and is rooted in the principle of party autonomy.

If the parties have agreed on a sole arbitrator instead of an arbitral tribunal, the appointment procedure is different. Obviously, it would not make any sense if both parties selected and nominated their own arbitrator and simply hoped that they both chose the same person. Rather, the parties have to reach an agreement on a sole arbitrator within the time limit stipulated in the applicable procedural rules. For example, under Article 7 of Annex 5 of the DIS Rules, the time limit is 30 days after receipt of the statement of claim by the respondent. A much shorter time limit of only 10 days is stipulated under Article 17 (3) of the SCC Rules. If the parties fail to jointly appoint the sole arbitrator, the decision lies with the arbitration institution as appointing authority (*cf.* Article 12(3) of the ICC Rules; Article 10.2 of the SIAC Rules).

Moreover, under many national arbitration laws, the parties are free to deviate from the above-mentioned procedure (*cf.* Article 11 (2) of the Model Law, Section 1035 (1) of the German Code of Civil Procedure). They could, for example, agree to appoint their arbitrators by drawing lots: Both parties could put five names in a hat and afterwards draw one each in order to nominate their co-arbitrators. However, the appointment procedure must meet basic requirements of procedural fairness and must not be completely to the advantage of one party over the other. This means that the third name, i.e. the president, must not be drawn by one of the parties but by a neutral third person. Since there is hardly any benefit to appointing arbitrators by drawing lots (except maybe for the joy of the draw), such individual appointment procedures are not found in practice. Rather, parties rely on the above-mentioned procedure which all relevant arbitration institutions conduct in a similar manner.

Finally, the importance of following the appointment procedure becomes clear when looking at the very end of an arbitration, i.e. the setting aside or enforcement of an award. According to Article 36 (1) lit. a (iv) of the Model Law, an award may be set aside if

> "the composition of the arbitral tribunal [...] was not in accordance with the agreement of the parties or, failing such agreement, was not in accordance with the law of the country where the arbitration took place"

(*cf.* also Section 1059 (2) No. 1 lit. d of the German Code of Civil Procedure). Clearly, this end does not justify the means of an individual appointment procedure!

3. AN APPOINTING AUTHORITY CAN BE IMPORTANT FOR THE PERFORMANCE OF THE ARBITRATION AGREEMENT

Arbitration agreements serve the purpose of enabling the parties to have their disputes decided in the agreed manner, i. e. by way of arbitration. An arbitration agreement that cannot be performed is useless for the parties. But when is this actually the case? This is usually the case if it is impossible to conduct the arbitral proceedings as agreed by the parties in the arbitration agreement. While one could think of many things that fit into this broad category, two aspects in particular stand out: What happens if one party simply refuses to nominate an arbitrator? Or what if the two co-arbitrators cannot agree on a president? Does this mean that it is impossible to conduct the arbitral proceedings because there is no arbitral tribunal?

The answer to this last question is straightforward: of course not! Arbitration would be a toothless tiger if one party could torpedo the process by simply refusing to participate. This is why all national arbitration laws and institutional rules provide a mechanism to deal with such situations: the appointing authority.

The appointing authority is a neutral body that steps in if something goes wrong during the process of establishing the arbitral tribunal. In cases where the parties have agreed on an arbitration administered by an arbitration institution, this institution provides the appointing authority. For example, Article 12.1 sentence 2 DIS Rules states:

> "If a party fails to nominate a co-arbitrator, such co-arbitrator shall be selected by the Appointing Committee and appointed pursuant to Article 13.2."

The DIS Appointing Committee also steps in if the co-arbitrators cannot agree on a president (Article 12.3 sentence 1 of the DIS Rules). All other arbitration institutions provide comparable services as appointing authorities (*cf.* Article 12 (4) of the ICC Rules). The institutions charge a modest fee for their services.

Important to know is the fact that institutions can hardly ever give reasons for their choice of an arbitrator when they act as appointing authority. As disappointing as this might be from a practitioner´s perspective, it makes sense since the parties are not acting cooperatively here. However, this lack of justification does not give a party any grounds to challenge the decision. And there is a good reason for this: even the parties need not give reasons for their choice of an arbitrator. As long as the appointed arbitrator is independent and impartial (and meets other specific requirements that the parties agreed upon, e. g. "*all arbitrators have to be state judges*"), it would be difficult for the parties to prove any legitimate interest in disclosure by the appointing authority of the reasons for the decision.

Furthermore, parties can also agree on individuals who will act as the appointing authority, e. g. the president of their favorite football team. Most important here is that both parties trust the chosen individual. However, our experience in international arbitration shows that there is little or no benefit for the parties to agree on an individual as appointing authority; individuals clearly do not have the same competence and focus as specialized arbitration institutions. So, this might be a rather theoretical aspect at least.

Finally, many national arbitration laws provide for an appointing authority for *ad hoc* arbitrations or in cases where the arbitration institution itself is unable or unwilling to fulfill its duty. The appointing authorities under the national laws are, not surprisingly, the state courts. Article 11 (5) of the Model Law allows each party to "*request the court [...] to take the necessary measure*", i. e. make the appointment (cf. also Section 1035 (4) of the German Code of Civil Procedure). The courts also protect the arbitration agreement if the parties made a mistake when drafting it, e. g. referred to a non-existent arbitration institution. In such cases, courts generally tend to uphold the agreement, if at all possible.

All in all, the appointing authority is essential for the performance of an arbitration agreement. The mere fact that there is an appointing authority in the process assures the parties that their arbitration agreement can be properly enforced. Neither party must fear that the opposing party may deprive it of the negotiated dispute resolution process by simply refusing to nominate an arbitrator.

4. YOUR BEST FRIEND MIGHT NOT BE YOUR BEST ARBITRATOR

"Pick arbitration, it is great, you can choose your own arbitrator!" Probably all in-house counsel have been told this or something similar about arbitration. And it is true: the possibility to choose your own arbitrator is an important advantage of arbitration over state court litigation. But who should be chosen, and what needs to be considered?

First of all, a party must not take the arbitrator selection lightly. The importance of this decision cannot be overstated. Again: the selection of an arbitrator is probably the most important decision to make in an arbitration. Second, the selection should be a decision based on experience and research. Already a quick internet search can reveal a lot about a possible arbitrator, and the experience of external counsel who know arbitrators from different cases is priceless. Third, it would be foolish to simply select a best friend as an arbitrator. A best friend will certainly not be the best arbitrator (or at the very least, they might not be a best friend for much longer)! The advantage of selecting an arbitrator is that one can choose the best expert for a case; it is not that you can simply pick someone you like. All arbitrators – without exceptions – must be fully independent and impartial!

There are many points a party should consider when choosing its arbitrator. Some are obvious, others might easily be forgotten. For example, the *expertise* and *qualification* of an arbitrator are aspects that anyone would naturally consider. Arbitrators should be experts with the right level of qualifications. The same is true for the *experience* and *competence* of a candidate. Arbitrators should have sufficient experience to handle a dispute in a competent manner. But what about an arbitrator's *availability*? What good is it to a case if a chosen arbitrator cannot give the appropriate attention to the dispute because he or she has too many other parallel cases? Another example is the arbitrator's *diligence*. In factual or legally complex cases that require an extra-diligent review of the case file, parties probably want to avoid having CEOs/top level managers as arbitrators who are used to only reviewing condensed information. A third example is the *nationality* of an arbitrator, especially in international cases. Arbitration institutions commonly refuse to appoint a president that shares the nationality of one but not both of the parties or co-arbitrators. Such aspects are crucial to consider.

Furthermore, parties should consider how effective an arbitrator would likely be in working with other members of the arbitral tribunal. An arbitral tribunal is never a one-man (or woman) show! And after all, arbitrators are humans, not robots (luckily not yet, with all the new Legal Tech developments). Social skills can be as important as expertise and qualifications. Every in-house counsel certainly agrees that it is easier to work together with someone who has a certain level of social skills.

However, this introduction should not be misunderstood as a statement that arbitrators' sympathies are irrelevant or that parties should even try to find arbitrators they dislike on a personal level. It is fair game in arbitration to select an arbitrator who is generally sympathetic to the party that nominated him or her. Or in the words of a seasoned English arbitration practitioner … who sadly passed away recently:

> "Indeed, when I am representing a client in an arbitration, what I am really looking for in a party-nominated arbitrator is someone with the maximum predisposition towards my client, but with the minimum appearance of bias."
>
> *(M. Hunter, Ethics of the International Arbitrator, ASA Bulletin 1986, 173, 189).*

The co-arbitrators´ job is to ensure that the arguments of the party appointing him or her are heard amongst the members of the tribunal. As such, it is standard practice for party-appointed arbitrators to appear a bit more favourable to "their party". This is part of the benefit of choosing an arbitrator. Equally, procedural safeguards exist to prohibit abuse, such as the possibility of challenging an arbitrator. Finally, parties hire arbitrators and pay for their services. No party can be forced to voluntarily work with a person they dislike

5. JUSTICE MUST NOT ONLY BE DONE, BUT BE SEEN TO BE DONE

Arbitration stands and falls with the parties' trust in the procedure as a dispute resolution mechanism. If parties do not trust the procedure, they will not use it! But when do parties trust the procedure? When they see that justice is done.

Justice can only be seen to be done if arbitrators are fully independent and completely impartial. Independence means that arbitrators do not take orders from anybody involved in the arbitration. An impartial arbitrator is unbiased. Both requirements are deeply rooted in the history of arbitration. Without them, arbitration could not exist! But while this is the international consensus, the manifestations of these concepts vary between national systems and institutional rules.

Article 12 (1) of the Model Law requires that a person called upon as an arbitrator must disclose all circumstances likely to give rise to justifiable doubts as to his or her impartiality or independence (*cf.* also Section 1036 (1) of the German Code of Civil Procedure). This obligation also includes such circumstances that arise after the appointment as arbitrator. The standard of impartiality and independence is an objective standard that does not require proof of certainty. In comparison, the Federal Arbitration Act (FAA), i. e. the US arbitration law, only addresses the arbitrator's impartiality when dealing with the grounds for setting aside the award. § 10 (a) (2) of the FAA requires that "*there was evident partiality or corruption in the arbitrators, or either of them*". This standard is relatively robust, making it more difficult for parties to challenge an arbitrator's impartiality.

During the arbitration process, independence and impartiality are guaranteed by the following three aspects:

First and foremost, arbitrators must disclose all circumstances that could give rise to doubts as to their impartiality or independence (*cf.* Article 9.4 sentence 2 of the DIS Rules). Most arbitration institutions send disclosure templates to the arbitrators which the arbitrators fill out and in which they can list relevant circumstances. Some institutions also request the parties to provide a list of companies and persons which the arbitrators must consider for their conflict checks. When drawing-up such a list as an in-house counsel, keep in mind that the longer and more detailed the list is the more likely are there going to be conflicts. This might make it difficult to find a good arbitrator.

It can be difficult for arbitrators to decide which circumstances need to be disclosed and in which cases disclosure is not necessary. In this respect, the IBA

Guidelines on Conflict of Interest in International Arbitration 2014 provide guidance ("IBA Guidelines"). The IBA Guidelines function as a soft law industry standard. They are recognised internationally and widely considered. In general, parties are well advised to encourage their arbitrator nominee to disclose all relevant circumstances. In doing so, they minimize the risk of subsequent discussions and further proceedings about the validity of the award which could in the end render the entire arbitration proceeding a fruitless endeavor.

Second, under all institutional arbitration rules, the parties have the right to object to a proposed arbitrator or to challenge an arbitrator (*cf.* Article 14 of the ICC Rules; Article 10.3 of the LCIA Rules). This is important to ensure procedural justice. Parties don't have to accept arbitrators who fail to meet the standard of impartiality and independence.

Third, a lack of neutrality of the tribunal can give grounds for parties to apply to the state courts to have an award set aside or can be raised against the enforcement of an award (*cf.* § 10 (a) (2) of the FAA). Of course, neither party must accept a decision rendered by a partial or biased arbitrator. However, a party may not withhold its doubts as to an arbitrator's independence or impartiality until after the award has been rendered. Most modern arbitration laws and institutional rules require that a party immediately raises its objections. In this case, the tribunal, the institution and/or courts might tackle the issue. Otherwise, the party runs the risk of being precluded later on.

6. CHALLENGE AN ARBITRATOR ONLY IF ABSOLUTELY NECESSARY

The possibility to challenge an arbitrator is an important part of the arbitral process. By agreeing on arbitration, parties waive their right to have their case decided by the legally competent judge. This is only possible because arbitrators must be independent and impartial (see III. 5). If a party believes that an arbitrator is biased, that party must be granted the procedural right to raise its concerns, i. e. to challenge the arbitrator. This is a basic principle under the rule of law. All legal systems provide for the possibility to challenge judges.

All arbitration institutions provide the parties with mechanisms to challenge arbitrators. For example, Article 14 (1) of the ICC Rules reads:

> "A challenge of an arbitrator, whether for an alleged lack of impartiality or independence, or otherwise, shall be made by the submission to the Secretariat of a written statement specifying the facts and circumstances on which the challenge is based".

Virtually identical provisions are contained in the DIS Rules, the LCIA Rules, and the rules of any other relevant arbitration institution. Most, if not all, institutional rules require a challenge to be filed with the institution, which then informs the challenged arbitrator. The institutional rules provide for a body which decides on a challenge. Under the ICC Rules, the ICC Secretariat decides on challenges, under the DIS Rules, the arbitration council makes this decision (*cf.* Article 15.4 of the DIS Rules). This ensures a proper process of dealing with a challenge.

Moreover, the institutions do not generally give reasons for their decisions. Often a party will not know why its challenge was denied or why an arbitrator was replaced. While this is sad from a practitioner´s perspective, it protects the process of handling arbitrator challenges. This is of course much more important. The only exception is the London Court of International Arbitration ("LCIA"). The LCIA by default gives reasons for its decisions in order to make the process transparent for the parties.

A different question, however, is whether and when it makes sense to challenge an arbitrator. Here the parties are well advised to challenge an arbitrator only when this is absolutely necessary, i. e. only in cases where the bias is written on the arbitrator's forehead. This is because, first, arbitrator challenges are hardly ever successful. A statistic from the Stockholm Chamber of Commerce from 2016 shows that almost 70 % of all challenges are rejected. The institutions are reluctant to grant challenges because any sustained challenge restricts a party's right to choose its arbitrator. This is of paramount importance and must not be seen likely.

Second, unless the strategy is to torpedo the process, challenges always disrupt and delay the arbitration. As a rule, the challenged arbitrator and the opposing party are given the opportunity to comment on a challenge in writing. This can easily take up to one month or longer. Then, the institution must decide on the challenge, which further delays the proceedings. Furthermore, if the challenge is finally successful, the parties and the tribunal must find a substitute arbitrator before they can continue the arbitration. An important aspect of arbitration – namely a speedy dispute resolution – would be endangered.

Finally, it should also be considered that arbitrators might see a challenge as a personal affront. Especially in the event of an unsuccessful challenge, a party may lose the goodwill of the tribunal. This at least does not make the further proceedings any easier for this party. The tribunal will often be stricter, for example on procedural issues where the tribunal has discretion, such as requests for the extension of a deadline. As such, challenges must be carefully considered and discussed with external counsel.

In summary, this does not mean that parties should never challenge an arbitrator. Parties should simply be cautious before challenging an arbitrator and only do so as a last resort.

7. APPOINTMENT OF ARBITRATORS IN MULTI-PARTY DISPUTES IS DIFFICULT AT BEST

Imagine the following scenario: a company enters into a consortium agreement for a new project with two other companies. Just before signing the agreement after intense contract negotiations, the lawyers include a standard ICC arbitration clause for an arbitral tribunal with three arbitrators. They recall that the possibility to choose the arbitrators is one of the advantages of arbitration over state court proceedings.

During the project, what has to happen happens: one of the consortium members regrets the agreement and initiates arbitration proceedings against the other consortium members. Following standard practice, the claimant nominates its arbitrator. Now what do the other consortium members do? The answer is easy: each of the consortium members selects and nominates an arbitrator; after all, this is one of the reasons why the companies have agreed to arbitration. Only now does each party realize that the other consortium member probably does exactly the same. And the chances that both parties choose the same arbitrator are slim. But what happens now? There are at least three possible scenarios:

First, the arbitration institution could step in and appoint an arbitrator for both respondents. While this might appear as the logical solution at first, hardly any institution would do this. The reason for this is the equal treatment of the parties, an extremely important principle in arbitration. The violation of equal treatment renders an award unenforceable. Here, the claimant could exercise the right to choose an arbitrator, but the respondents could not. The appointment of the arbitrator for the respondents by the institution leads to an advantage of the claimant, i. e. the parties are treated unequally.

Second, each party could be allowed to exercise its right to appoint its own arbitrator. Three parties, three arbitrators. However, this only works if there are not more than three parties involved. What if there are four, five or maybe eight consortium members? This would also mean that the tribunal has no neutrally appointed president. Having one of the party-appointed arbitrators as chair would give this party an advantage over the others, i. e. this could again be seen as a violation of equal treatment. The only other alternative that has come up in practice would be to increase the number of arbitrators from three to five. Then the three party-appointed arbitrators would agree on two presidents. However, courts have found that this would violate the parties' arbitration agreement (*cf. BP Exploration Libya Ltd. v. ExxonMobil Libya Ltd.*).

Third, the arbitration institution could take over completely and appoint both co-arbitrators as well as determine the president. In this way, all parties would be treated equally, since everyone would lose the chance to choose an arbitrator. However, is it not at least questionable that the claimant should lose its right solely because the respondents were unable to agree on a joint arbitrator? Nevertheless, most arbitration institutions and national arbitration laws follow this approach. For example, Article 12 (8) of the ICC Rules states that

> "[i]n the absence of a joint nomination [...] the Court [= the arbitral institution, scil] may appoint each member of the arbitral tribunal and shall designate one of them to act as president".

All in all, none of the three scenarios described above is fully convincing. Yet, only the last scenario takes into account that in this difficult situation it is of paramount importance that all parties are treated equally. Therefore, all the parties are deprived of their right to choose an arbitrator, and the institution or the court appoints the entire tribunal in order to ensure equal treatment. This is important for in-house counsel (and external M&A/corporate lawyers) to keep in mind when drafting-up agreements. Because the principle of party-autonomy gives party the freedom to deal and resolve this issue long before a dispute is on the horizon.

8. "BECAUSE I SAY SO!" – ARBITRATORS HAVE GREAT DISCRETION IN RUNNING THE PROCEEDINGS

Arbitration allows the parties to choose the procedural rules for their dispute. Theoretically, the parties could write down an entire procedural code for their proceedings. However, this never happens in practice. Doing so would be unnecessarily time-consuming, or in other words: a waste of time and money. Rather, the parties simply refer to the procedural framework provided by the rules of the arbitration institutions. Rightly so.

All major institutions provide well-balanced procedural rules. Under these rules, arbitrators generally have a wide discretion to run the proceedings, which is only limited by express agreements between the parties and few (but important) mandatory due process rules (e.g. procedural fairness and equal treatment of the parties). In this regard, it is fair to say that the arbitrators are the real masters of the proceedings. For example, Article 19.1 of the SIAC Rules states that

> "[t]he Tribunal shall conduct the arbitration in such manner as it considers appropriate, after consulting with the parties, to ensure the fair, expeditious, economical and final resolution of the dispute".

The arbitrators define what *appropriate* means. Parties do have an influence though, provided that they agree on certain procedural issues.

The rationale behind the arbitrators' wide discretion is procedural efficiency. In order to make arbitration an efficient dispute resolution method, arbitrators must be able to conduct proceedings in a way that meets the needs of the particular case. This is the reason why most national arbitration laws also stipulate that the arbitrators run the proceedings at their discretion, in the absence of an express party agreement. Article 19 (2) of the Model Law states that failing a party agreement,

> "the arbitral tribunal may [...] conduct the arbitration in such manner as it considers appropriate"

(cf. also Section 1042 (4) of the German Code of Civil Procedure).

When exercising their discretion, arbitrators should consider the legal background of the parties and the circumstances of the individual case. This means that in an arbitration where both parties come from civil law countries, it would make sense for the arbitrators to apply civil law procedural rules, whereas in cases where the parties come from civil law and common law countries, i. e. truly international proceedings, tribunals often rely on a mixture of rules from both systems.

In practice, arbitrators make use of their discretion by way of procedural orders. These are the primary tools for arbitrators to structure the proceedings. Procedural orders, for example, contain rules about *(i)* notifications and communications between the parties and the tribunal, *(ii)* timing, number and length of written submissions, and *(iii)* the way parties have to submit evidence in the proceedings. Seasoned and experienced arbitrators all have templates for such procedural orders at hand. During the course of the arbitration, tribunals issue procedural orders on many different topics, e. g. the amount in dispute. Arbitral tribunals generally consult with the parties before issuing a procedural order. However, especially for arbitrations seated in Germany, arbitrators have to be careful to always make crystal clear that their procedural orders are not based on an agreement between the parties. Otherwise, arbitrators might be unable to change or adapt the procedural rules during the course of the proceedings without running the risk that the award might be challenged in the end on the grounds that the tribunal deviated from the parties' agreement (*cf.* Higher Regional Court Frankfurt a. M., 17 February 2011, 26 Sch 13/10). In-house counsel need to be aware of this in order not to run the risk that the opposing party applies for a setting-aside of the award.

Finally, this risk of creating an unenforceable award is also the reason why arbitrators are rarely tough on procedural issues. As mentioned, arbitrators generally consult with the parties and try to reach a consensus about the procedural rules. Indeed, this makes sense because it is only possible to conduct an efficient arbitration if both parties agree with the chosen procedure. To this end, the following saying sums up the arbitrators' position best: *When in doubt, hear them out!*

9. THE LIABILITY OF ARBITRATORS IS USUALLY LIMITED

Arbitrators render their services to the parties on the basis of a contract, the so-called arbitrator's contract. This means that the civil liability of arbitrators by its nature concerns contractual liability (further liability of arbitrators may be based on tort or criminal liability). The legal standard for the liability of arbitrators is straightforward: like any contractual liability, it requires: (*i*) a breach of contract; (*ii*) damage caused to one (or both) of the parties; and (*iii*) a causal link between the breach of contract and the damage. The arbitrator must be responsible for his or her breach of contract, which is legally assumed in various jurisdictions (e.g. Section 280 (1) Sentence 2 of the German Civil Code or Article 97 (1) of the Swiss Code of Obligations).

When talking about the liability of arbitrators, two cases should be distinguished: (*i*) liability for actions in connection with deciding on a legal matter; and (*ii*) liability for other acts or omissions in connection with the arbitral proceedings.

First, arbitrators might be liable for actions in connection with deciding on a legal matter. This means that parties might consider holding an arbitrator liable due to the performance of his or her adjudicative function. In other words: The losing party could try to argue that the arbitrator made a "wrong decision". Such a "wrong decision" would then constitute a breach of contract and entitle said party to damages from the arbitrator.

Second, arbitrators might also be liable for acts or omissions in connection with the arbitral proceedings, i.e. non-adjudicative acts. Arbitrators might be liable for organizational acts relating to the oral hearing, for example, if they fail to promptly inform the parties about the venue of the hearing.

However, arbitrators can generally rely on immunity from civil claims of the parties. Almost all jurisdictions grant arbitrators with some form of immunity, either by statutory or by common law. For example, Section 25 of the Singapore International Arbitration Act (Chapter 143 A) provides that

> "[a]n arbitrator shall not be liable for (a) negligence in respect of anything done or omitted to be done in the capacity of arbitrator; and (b) any mistake in law, fact or procedure made in the course of arbitral proceedings or in the making of an arbitral award".

US courts have held that arbitrators are immune from civil liability for all acts performed in their arbitral capacity (*Austern v. Chicago Board Options Exchange*).

The Model Law (as well as German arbitration law) does not provide for immunity. But this does not mean that arbitrators in Germany would face civil claims without any limitation of liability. Arbitrators can rely by analogy on Section 839 (2) of the German Civil Code which provides that "*if an official breaches his official duties in a judgement in a legal matter, then he is only responsible for any damage arising from this if the breach of duty consists in a criminal offence*". Arbitrators are, thus, largely immune from civil claims for their adjudicative acts under German law. However, German law does not provide for immunity for non-adjudicative acts.

Furthermore, all relevant institutional arbitration rules limit the liability of arbitrators. For example, the ICC Rules in Article 41 provide that

> "[T]he arbitrators, [...] shall not be liable to any person for any act or omission in connection with the arbitration, except to the extent such limitation of liability is prohibited by applicable law".

Another example is Article 45 of the DIS Rules. In particular, Article 45.2 of the DIS Rules excludes liability

> "For any other acts or omissions in connection with the arbitration, an arbitrator, the DIS, its statutory organs, its employees, and any other person associated with the DIS who is involved in the arbitration shall not be liable, except in case of an intentional breach of duty or gross negligence."

The DIS Rules thus extend the immunity of arbitrators to non-adjudicative acts. This immunity, however, does not cover intentional or grossly negligent breaches because of mandatory restraints under domestic German law.

Another aspect that is increasingly coming into focus is the liability of arbitration institutions. While arbitration institutions in common law countries quite frequently find themselves exposed to civil claims from dissatisfied parties, parties to arbitration in civil law countries have hardly ever raised any claims against arbitration institutions. In any case, most institutional arbitration rules extend immunity to the arbitration institution and its staff (*cf.* Article 45.2 of the DIS Rules; Article 31.1 of the LCIA Rules; Article 52 of the SCC Rules). Parties agree to these immunities when they commence an arbitration administered by the respective institution.

10. EMERGENCY ARBITRATOR: SOMETIMES A RULING IS REQUIRED BEFORE THE ARBITRATION STARTS

A rather new phenomenon in international arbitration is the emergency arbitrator. Originally, a party was unable to obtain any arbitral relief before the arbitral tribunal was fully constituted, because only the arbitral tribunal has the power to render judicial decisions. The arbitration institutions do not have this power. However, the constitution of the arbitral tribunal can be a time-consuming process which often takes months. During this time, a party in need of judicial relief has no choice but to apply to state courts for interim relief. This is problematic because one of the reasons for parties to agree to arbitration is that parties want to derogate from state courts. To solve this problem, the arbitral community came up with the idea of an emergency arbitrator.

The rationale behind the emergency arbitrator mechanism is a one-stop-shop principle for arbitral relief. The purpose of the emergency arbitrator is to enable a request for an interim measure prior to and after the commencement of the arbitration, but before the case has been referred to the arbitral tribunal. In other words, the emergency arbitrator mechanism is a form of interim measure or interim relief available to the parties. If a party needs immediate legal relief, an emergency arbitrator can often provide it. A possible scenario for such immediate relief could be a party that fears that the opposing party could destroy essential evidence in its possession. The emergency arbitrator mechanism was first adopted by the International Center for Dispute Resolution (ICDR) in 2006 and has since been followed by most major arbitration institutions (*cf.* Article 29 of the ICC Rules; Article 9B of the LCIA Rules; Article 30 of the SIAC Rules).

Three key features of emergency arbitrator proceedings are:

1. Default application: Emergency arbitrator provisions apply by default. By choosing the rules of an arbitration institution that has adopted emergency arbitrator provisions, both parties can apply for emergency measures even if they have not expressly agreed on them. In contrast, most institutional rules follow an opt-out approach, which means that parties expressly have to opt out of the emergency arbitrator provisions.
2. Express appointment and procedure: Emergency arbitrator proceedings must, by their nature, be conducted quickly. Therefore, the institution ap-

points the emergency arbitrator instead of the parties. For example, the ICC appoints the emergency arbitrator within the shortest possible time, normally within two days (Article 2 (1) of Appendix V of the ICC Rules). The entire proceedings must then take place within 15 days from the date on which the file was transmitted to the emergency arbitrator.

3. Wide discretion: Emergency arbitrators' decisions are based on a summary assessment of the case. There is not yet a universal test setting out the requirements for urgent pre-arbitral relief; nevertheless, emergency arbitrators will generally consider (*a*) whether a party will suffer irreparable harm if the requested relief is not granted, (*b*) whether such harm substantially outweighs the harm imposed on the other party by the interim measure, and (*c*) whether the requesting party has a reasonable chance of succeeding on the merits. The emergency arbitrator has wide discretion in this regard.

Perhaps one of the hottest topics in international arbitration at the moment is the enforcement of emergency arbitrators' decisions. Since the entire mechanism is rather new, there has been only a limited number of cases where the parties have tried to enforce such decisions. The legal nature of emergency arbitrators and their decisions can at best be described as unclear. The main problem is that under the New York Convention, only arbitral awards are recognizable and enforceable whereas purely procedural orders cannot be enforced. State courts have treated the question of whether or not interim measures are awards inconsistently. However, the tendency is clearly in favor of enforcing emergency arbitrators' decisions, i. e. accepting them as awards under the New York Convention. This development could boost the number of emergency arbitrator applications because it provides parties with (at least some) legal certainty regarding the usefulness of emergency proceedings.

IV.

THE ARBITRAL PROCEEDINGS

1. THERE ARE SEVEN COMMON STEPS IN ARBITRAL PROCEEDINGS

In arbitral proceedings, the parties are free to agree on the procedure, and where the parties have not agreed on specific rules, the tribunal has wide discretion as to how to structure the proceedings (*cf.* for example Articles 19 and 20 of the ICC Rules). Nevertheless, there are certain steps which most arbitral proceedings have in common:

Step #1: Initiation of the Proceeding. The claimant in an arbitration must first formally initiate the arbitral proceeding. The claimant has to submit a request for arbitration or a statement of claim. This step is required to inform the other party about the arbitration so that the other party can appoint its arbitrator (if foreseen under the applicable rules), decide on the future course of action and submit its arguments. The request for arbitration must therefore be served on the respondent. The required content of a request for arbitration depends on the parties' agreement and the applicable statutory laws at the seat of the arbitration. If the parties have agreed on the arbitration rules of an arbitration institution, these rules provide detailed guidance on the minimum content of the request for arbitration. It is at least necessary to identify the parties as well as the relief sought and to briefly describe the facts of the case. Only when such information is available is it possible to determine the parties to the arbitration and the subject matter of the dispute. If the parties have not agreed on specific rules, the statutory arbitration laws apply, usually providing for similar rules (*cf.* Article 23 (1) of the Model Law).

Step #2: Constitution of the Arbitral Tribunal. In arbitration, a permanent tribunal usually does not exist. Therefore, the tribunal must first be constituted. It is an advantage of arbitration that the parties can choose the arbitrators so that they can appoint someone who has specific expertise in the relevant field of law or otherwise of the subject matter in dispute (for details see III. 1. – 4.).

Step #3: Determination of Procedural Rules. When the tribunal is constituted, the tribunal familiarizes itself with the request for arbitration (and potentially also with the first submission of the respondent). In a case management conference, the tribunal will determine the specific rules of the proceedings and the provisional timetable. The case management conference helps to structure the proceedings and to increase the efficiency of the arbitration. While the ICC Rules contain the specific order to the tribunal to conduct a case management conference ("shall", Article 24 of the ICC Rules), other rules, such as those of the AAA, stress the tribunal's discretion in this respect (Article 21 of the AAA Rules). The tribunal will determine formalities, such as how submissions are to be filed, how evidence is to be submitted, and how many rounds of written submission are to take place. In essence, the tribunal has the possibility to set the course for more "German" proceedings with a strong "inquisitorial" tribunal. In the alternative, the tribunal could adopt a rather Anglo-American approach and have the parties submit written witness statements, have cross-examinations in the hearing, etc.

Step #4: Exchange of Written Submissions. Tribunals often order two full rounds of submissions: full statement of claim, full statement of defense, statement of reply, and statement of rejoinder. This gives the parties ample opportunity to make their case.

Step #5: Taking of Evidence and Oral Hearing. There are different categories of evidence that can be presented to tribunals: documentary evidence, witness evidence, experts as well as inspections of the subject matter of the dispute. Especially the disclosure of documents plays an important role in international arbitral proceedings.

Unless the parties have agreed upon "documents only", hearings will be the next step. Convening pre-hearing conferences is common practice and part of the tribunal's general discretion. In the pre-hearing conference, the tribunal organizes the oral hearing together with the parties. In the oral hearing, the parties usually deliver their opening statements, followed by witness and expert examinations. It is common that a court reporter is present and produces a verbatim transcript of the entire hearing.

Step #6: Exchange of Post-Hearing Submissions. The tribunal has two options to terminate the arbitral proceedings: (*a*) The tribunal may instruct the parties to hold closing pleadings at the end of the oral hearing. (*b*) The tribunal may instruct the parties to submit one or two post-hearing briefs each. In such briefs, the parties summarize their main arguments and the result of the witness and expert examination during the oral hearing, or they answer questions raised by the tribunal. At this stage, the tribunal usually requests that the parties submit their cost submissions.

Step #7: Rendering and Enforcing the Arbitral Award. The arbitration proceeding ends with the arbitral award. The arbitral award is usually final and binding and cannot be appealed. The arbitral award is enforceable under the New York Convention in almost all countries of the world.

2. THE TERMS OF REFERENCE PROVIDE A GUIDING HAND

Terms of reference are a case management mechanism that is almost unique to the ICC Rules. The term refers to a document that the tribunal has to prepare pursuant to Article 23 of the ICC Rules. None of the other major arbitration institutions have included an obligation to set up terms of reference in their arbitration rules.

The terms of reference contain a wealth of information, ranging from the contact details of the parties and the arbitrators to procedural and substantive agreements. The parties and the tribunal will usually identify and agree on procedural matters, such as the applicable law, the language, place and timetable of the proceeding as well as other particulars of the applicable procedural rules. The same applies to substantive issues. The terms of reference must contain a summary of the parties' respective claims and reliefs sought, and the tribunal and the parties will try to reach agreement on the substantive issues to be addressed in the arbitration. When setting up the terms of reference, the tribunal narrows down the dispute and the topics that are to be addressed by the parties. The parties may not introduce new claims that are outside the limits of the terms of reference, unless they have been authorized to do so by the arbitral tribunal.

The tribunal will prepare the terms of reference either on the basis of documents or in the presence of the parties, but always in light of the parties' submissions (usually based on the claimant's request for arbitration and the respondent's answer). While the arbitral tribunal has the ultimate responsibility for setting up the terms of reference, they are usually prepared in a collaborative way with the parties being actively involved. Typically, the tribunal prepares a first draft of the terms of reference and sends it to the parties in order to obtain their comments and feedback. The finalized document must be signed by the parties.

Legally, the terms of reference are a "real" agreement which binds the arbitrators and the parties. Therefore, the arbitral tribunal is not entitled to deviate from the rules contained in the terms of reference without the approval of all parties involved. If the tribunal violates the agreement, the arbitral award might be challenged later on. Therefore, tribunals and parties are careful not to include too many issues in the terms of reference, but to have them ordered by the tribunal in separate procedural orders.

By signing, the parties declare that they agree with the dispute to be resolved through arbitration and with the due constitution of the arbitral tribunal. Unless the parties expressly reserve their right to do so when signing the terms of reference, they may not argue the invalidity of the arbitration agreement or the undue constitution of the arbitral tribunal at a later stage.

While some critics reject the concept of terms of reference by arguing that they unnecessarily delay the proceedings, drive up costs, and increase bureaucracy at the outset of the proceedings, others recognize advantages in the terms of reference. Indeed, terms of reference serve various purposes: the cooperation and active involvement of the parties at such an early stage of the proceedings is the basis for a successful and cooperative approach with respect to the future proceedings. This allows for a faster and more efficient resolution of the dispute. In addition, clear terms of reference allow the parties and the tribunal to focus on the issues which were identified as being decisive. As already indicated in the heading, terms of reference serve as a guide to which the parties and the tribunal can refer throughout the proceedings. The terms of reference provide a clear structure at the outset of the proceedings, which will lead to fewer disputes concerning the conduct of the proceedings at a later stage. Unambiguous terms of reference are very likely to reduce the risk that the arbitral award will be vacated or that its recognition and enforcement will be denied; this is because they help ensure that the tribunal acts within its mandate throughout the proceedings and that the final award deals with all issues identified by the parties. Since the terms of reference are a mandatory requirement, the arbitrators and the parties are forced to determine the live issues of the dispute at an early stage. However, the terms of reference unfold their advantages only if they are taken seriously from the very outset of the proceedings and the tribunal and the parties do not merely use a standard template without considering the specific aspects of the case.

3. BIFURCATING PROCEEDINGS CAN SAVE COSTS FOR THE PARTIES

The term "bifurcation" literally means the division of something into two parts. Based on this, the division into different phases is what is also understood by bifurcation in the context of procedural law. The proceedings may be divided into a phase dealing with jurisdictional issues and a phase dealing with the merits of the case or, as is most commonly done, into a liability and a quantum phase. A third option, which is common practice in investment arbitration, is a trifurcation into jurisdictional, liability and quantum issues.

Yet, the substance and effects of bifurcation in the procedural law context are more far-reaching than indicated by the general linguistic usage. Bifurcated proceedings mean separated phases which are decided on separately. At the end of the first phase, the tribunal will render a partial award, which is enforceable as such, or a procedural order with its findings on this phase. The final award is then the result of the last phase. Bifurcation of arbitral proceedings is usually a decision made during one of the preliminary steps of the arbitration, such as the case management conference.

While bifurcation is increasingly used in arbitral proceedings, it is not explicitly mentioned in most institutional arbitration rules. In the absence of specific rules, the right to bifurcate the proceedings stems from the general flexibility and discretion the arbitral tribunal has in conducting the proceedings. Some rules, however, do mention bifurcation. The ICDR and AAA Rules expressly stipulate the right to bifurcate the proceedings in the main rules (Article 20.3 of the ICDR Rules; Article 23 of the AAA Rules). The ICC Rules of Arbitration do not specifically mention bifurcation in the main rules, but list it as a possible approach which the tribunal can adopt pursuant to Appendix IV of the ICC Rules.

Many disputes involve major discussions and efforts regarding the quantification of damages. This is particularly true for highly technical disputes in relation to intellectual property or construction projects. The quantification may involve large quantities of documents as well as a myriad of witnesses and/or expert witnesses. In such cases, bifurcation may save some of these efforts, depending on the tribunal's decision at the liability stage. If the tribunal decides that the respondent is not to be held liable for the alleged breach of contract, a quantification of the damages is superfluous, and the parties can save their submissions. A bifurcation may also be appropriate when settlement is likely or when the liability and quantum parts are significantly imbalanced. However, bifurcation does not always contribute to the efficiency of the proceedings. Since a bifurcation requires the parties to file additional submissions and to have at least one additional hearing, bifurcation may result in prolonged proceedings which are inevitably connected to higher costs. This is particularly the case when quantum-related topics are already relevant to determine the merits of the case, such as when one party argues that it can no longer be bound by a contract because it has suffered losses due to changed circumstances, and when the parties at the same time are discussing lost profits from a project. A tribunal should therefore decide whether to bifurcate on a case-by-case basis, taking into consideration all the circumstances of the individual case.

A tribunal might consider the following criteria when it decides on the bifurcation of arbitral proceedings: (*i*) a bifurcation of proceedings can be considered only when a separation of the issues is possible. If the issues are interwoven so that one issue can only be reasonably discussed in connection with the other issue, a tribunal should not bifurcate the proceedings. In such a constellation, bifurcation would inevitably cause doublings and repetitions in the different phases of the proceedings. The parties would have to address the issues which are connected to more than one phase again and again. Furthermore, the parties might want to re-open some of the issues that were discussed in the first phase but are also relevant to the later proceedings. However, the tribunal would not be allowed to deviate from its foregoing decision (if rendered as an arbitral award) – even if it would like to do so due to a better understanding of the issue. (*ii*) An arbitral tribunal may not order a bifurcation if the bifurcation would result in an unfair advantage to one party. This may be the case if the party's pleading is contradictory and bifurcation would help the party to uphold its argumentation.

4. WRITTEN SUBMISSIONS HAVE TO COMPLY WITH FORMAL AND MATERIAL REQUIREMENTS

Written submissions contain the basic legal claims, arguments and defenses of the parties. The statement of claim and statement of defense play a major role in arbitral proceedings. Typically, there are more than just two written submissions in arbitration. The parties usually file at least a statement of reply and a rejoinder. If the respondent raises counterclaims, the claimant must have the opportunity to reply to the counterclaims with further written submissions. In complex arbitral proceedings, the parties and the tribunal might wish to have additional rounds of written submissions in order to further elaborate on their arguments.

The parties to an arbitration are generally free to agree on requirements regarding their written submissions. However, there are some standards that apply to any arbitration: Each party must have the opportunity to be heard by the arbitrators, and *ex parte* communication must not take place. The latter rule obliges the parties and their representatives in an arbitration to refrain from *exclusive* communication about the substance of the case or otherwise with the arbitrators. The above basic rules are based on the internationally acknowledged principle of procedural fairness; they apply even in cases where there are no such written provisions available in the applicable law. Article 3 of the ICC Rules sets out the requirements of written notifications or communications as well as time limits. It stipulates that all pleadings and other written party communications must be supplied in sufficient numbers to provide one copy for each party and for each arbitrator (and sometimes also for the institution that administers the proceedings).

In the absence of a party agreement regarding the written submissions, the applicable law on arbitration at the seat of arbitration will usually provide some regulations. The UNCITRAL Model Law, for example, which has been used as a basis for many national laws, deals with written submissions in Article 23. It stipulates that either the parties or the tribunal may determine the time limits for the written submissions. Article 23 of the Model Law demands, *inter alia*, that the claimant state the facts supporting his claims, the issues in dispute, and the relief or remedy sought, and that the respondent set forth his defense in respect of these particulars (unless – of course – the parties have agreed otherwise as to the required elements of such statements).

Language is a formal aspect of written submissions. It is usually agreed upon by the parties. In the absence of such an agreement, the tribunal will determine the language of the arbitration and of the written submissions, taking into consideration the circumstances of the case.

Written submission are important for the outcome of the proceedings. In general, there are no page limits, and the written submissions may be quite long and complex. Content, form, and timing of written submissions vary from arbitration to arbitration. However, it is recommendable to avoid in written submissions the kind of empty words and formalisms that often enough prevail in domestic litigation. The parties should bear in mind that the tribunal is often composed of arbitrators with different cultural and legal backgrounds. Therefore, the parties are well advised to draft submissions that are understandable and persuasive to readers from any of the legal and linguistic backgrounds concerned.

There are no general rules as regards the timing of written submissions; this should be addressed on a case-by-case basis by the parties and the tribunal. As the case may be, it can be recommendable that the parties' submissions are submitted simultaneously, so neither party has an opportunity to formulate its position or argument in response to the other. In other cases, sequential submissions may be desirable and specifically provided for.

It is advisable for the tribunal to clarify what the sequence and timing of the parties' submissions should be, always taking into account the parties' rights to equal treatment and to be heard. The parties should agree on certain timing aspects, such as what "close of business" means and which particular time zone will be considered. The tribunal should also clarify what happens if a party files its submission too late or if it files an unsolicited submission. It frequently happens that a party files an unsolicited submission shortly before a hearing and the other party does not have enough time to analyze the new submission or establish whether it needs to reply. When this happens, the timetable of the arbitration is endangered, and efficient resolution of the dispute is impossible. If the tribunal has not made it clear that a time limit is binding and that a late submission will be rejected, the tribunal is often considered to be obliged to accept the late submission – with all the consequences for the timetable and the proceedings.

5. OBJECTIONS TO THE JURISDICTION HAVE TO BE RAISED QUICKLY

Jurisdictional issues are part of many disputes between parties to an arbitration. Doubts may arise as to whether a tribunal has the authority to decide certain claims submitted to it by the parties. The doubts may also concern the jurisdiction of the tribunal as a whole, *i. e.* whether the parties have validly agreed to refer their dispute to arbitration. A typical situation in which such a concern arises is when there is doubt about the validity of the substantive contract.

When it comes to challenging a tribunal's jurisdiction, there are two ways to do so: A respondent may either submit its challenge to the arbitral tribunal or file an application with the competent state court. Challenges submitted to an arbitral tribunal are dealt with by this tribunal. This is because arbitral tribunals have the preliminary competence to decide on their own jurisdiction (so-called *competence-competence*). However, such a decision may be subject to review by a state court which has the final say in this regard (e.g. if the arbitral award is challenged later on).

A tribunal must decide on a challenge submitted by a party only if the challenge was raised in due time. As a general rule, concerns as to the jurisdiction have to be raised prior to any pleadings on the merits. Otherwise, the parties are deemed to accept the arbitration or at least waive their right to challenge the jurisdiction for the remainder of the proceedings. Parties can avoid such a consequence by expressly reserving the right to challenge jurisdiction at a later stage.

Most institutional rules and arbitration laws provide for even stricter time limits, distinguishing between challenges as to a tribunal's jurisdiction and challenges concerning an exceedance of authority. Pursuant to these rules, challenges concerning the jurisdiction must be raised before any defense on the merits. In the case of jurisdictional concerns in connection with counterclaims, objections must be raised in the reply to the counterclaim. In contrast, the objection that the arbitral tribunal is exceeding its powers must be raised as soon as the alleged exceeding of powers has taken place in the arbitral proceedings. Such time limits are, for example, part of the regulation in Article 23.2 of the UNCITRAL Arbitration Rules. Identical provisions can be found in Article 16 (2) of the Model Law, Section 1040 (2) of the German Code of Civil Procedure, and Section 31 (2) of the UK Arbitration Act 1996. The LCIA provides for a similar regulation in Article 23.3 of the LCIA Rules. Other laws, such as the Swiss Arbitration Law, do not distinguish between the two types of challenge, but merely provide for challenges no later than any defense on the merits (Article 186 (2) of the Swiss Federal Statute on Private International Law). In any case and under any of these rules and laws, a tribunal may accept a later challenge if it considers the delay justified in the circumstances. This does not mean that a respondent should wait for the time limit to expire. An exception will always depend on the goodwill of the arbitral tribunal and cannot be predicted. Therefore, parties are well advised to raise any objections as to the jurisdiction or authority of a tribunal as soon as possible.

The second way is to file an application challenging the tribunal's jurisdiction with a state court. This is only possible where the local arbitration law permits such intervention by national courts. Depending on the respective laws, there are three possible points in time for doing so: at the beginning of the arbitral process, during the arbitral proceedings or after the rendering of the award. Nevertheless, if a respondent wishes to challenge the jurisdiction of the arbitral tribunal in court, it is highly advisable to do so as soon as possible and before the arbitral tribunal is constituted. Otherwise, the arbitration will proceed without regard to the pending challenge before the state courts. The respondent can raise the argument when it comes to the enforcement of the arbitral award under the New York Convention. An arbitral award is not enforceable if an arbitration agreement does not exist (and if the respondent had objected to the arbitration on time).

6. SET-OFF DEFENSES ARE ADMISSIBLE IN ARBITRAL PROCEEDINGS IF THE UNDERLYING CLAIM IS COVERED BY THE ARBITRATION AGREEMENT

If a respondent is confronted with a claim before an arbitral tribunal, it has three options at its disposal in order to defend itself. The most natural reaction is to reject the claimant's allegations. More on the offensive, the respondent can additionally submit a counterclaim. Thirdly, it can raise a set-off defense. As the latter is often confused with a counterclaim, it is important to work out the differences. A counterclaim is an independent and substantive claim brought by a respondent. It will be admissible only if it falls under the scope of the arbitration agreement which is usually the case if the counterclaim arises out of the same legal relationship as does the main claim and if it is directed against a party to the arbitration. Conversely, a set-off is an accessory (or dependent) defense to a claim. One may say that it serves as a shield being designed to unilaterally extinguish substantive obligations that exist between the parties. A set-off is limited up to the amount requested by the claimant.

If the respondent's claim exceeds that of the claimant, the surplus has to be raised in additional proceedings. The dependence further means that the set-off is invalid if the original claim is no longer due for any reason. An independent counterclaim will remain pending no matter what happens to the claims.

The nature, requirements and effect of set-off defenses vary among states. While most of the civil law jurisdictions treat set-offs as substantive, others treat them as procedural. Some even distinguish between various kinds of set-offs.

Apart from that, the question with respect to set-offs in arbitration is whether or not they are admissible. In this regard, one would expect that the law applicable to the arbitration agreement would provide some guidance. Yet with the exception of the Swiss Rules, the arbitration laws and institutional rules remain silent on the admissibility of set-offs. When assessing their admissibility, one has to differentiate between different procedural scenarios.

In a first scenario, the claim underlying the set-off is not covered by any other arbitration agreement or forum selection clause. The set-off is admissible only if the underlying claim is covered by the arbitration agreement between the parties.

Otherwise, a set-off is impossible because the arbitral tribunal lacks the competence to decide upon the existence of this claim. However, some arbitral tribunals have extended the admissibility of a set-off to "*closely related contracts*" such as a loan agreement which is intended to finance a purchase agreement. If the set-off claim is not covered by the agreement, the admissibility will depend on the reaction of the other party, *i. e.* whether the other party objects to the tribunal's authority to decide the case.

In a second scenario in which the claim underlying the arbitration agreement is subject to another arbitration agreement or forum selection clause, it becomes more difficult. Article 21.5 of the Swiss Rules reads:

> "The arbitral tribunal shall have jurisdiction to hear a set-off defence even if the relationship out of which the defence is said to arise is not within the scope of the arbitration clause, or falls within the scope of another arbitration agreement or forum-selection clause".

This is a pragmatic approach which is intended to increase procedural efficiency by admitting set-off claims even if they are covered by another arbitration agreement. The idea behind this is that mutual liabilities should not be part of different proceedings. However, in light of the various problems arising out of this, the provision is heavily contested. Two tribunals may decide on the same claim either subsequently or simultaneously. With respect to the former, questions arise as to whether a set-off declared by the first tribunal may establish *res judicata* effect or whether the second tribunal would be bound by that decision. If two tribunals decide concurrently, the question arises whether the rules of *lis pendens* may be applied in arbitral proceedings as well. In any case, this may lead to conflicting decisions which contradicts the purpose of procedural efficiency.

Therefore, such set-off defenses are generally to be considered inadmissible. Despite the differences, a set-off claim, just like a counterclaim, has to be covered by the arbitration agreement which is the foundation of any tribunal's jurisdiction and authority. Furthermore, the admissibility of a set-off would ignore the will of the parties as it is expressed by the other arbitration agreement or forum selection clause. Even if both of the agreements refer their respective disputes to the same institution, a set-off cannot be admissible as it would amount to a consolidation of proceedings, which, however, is only possible with the parties' express consent. As in international arbitration the will of the parties will always prevail over procedural efficiency; set-off claims which are not covered by the parties' agreement will thus be inadmissible. There are only a few exceptions. This is the case where the set-off claim is uncontested or where the claim has already been recognized by a declaratory judgement. It derives from the principle of good faith that a set-off claim is admissible where the counterparty does not object to the tribunal's jurisdiction to hear the claim. Lastly, the lack of jurisdiction with respect to a set-off claim can be cured due to a subsequent agreement of the parties submitting the claim to the arbitral tribunal.

7. CULTURE HAS AN IMPACT – THE "AMERICANIZATION" OF PROCEEDINGS

International arbitration developed primarily on the European continent, with France, Germany, and Switzerland participating in a significant number of cross-border arbitrations. The United States was not originally involved in this development. Thus, international commercial arbitration developed essentially as an adaptation of civil law rules of procedure rather than those of the common law known in the United States and England. However, international commercial arbitration has undergone a radical change over the past fifty years. The United States and England are important places for litigation. And so it comes as no surprise that nowadays, both the United States and England are similarly involved in international arbitration. American lawyers participating in international commercial arbitration brought and used American litigation skills in arbitration when they arrived in Europe in the 1970s to represent their clients in large petroleum arbitrations.

Therefore, moving towards an American style of litigation became the new trend in international arbitration. Some would even say that arbitration has turned into a kind of "offshore litigation". Without going so far, the "Americanization" can be shown by the adoption of methods and procedures commonly used in American litigation, such as cross-examination, interviewing of witnesses, depositions, and so forth. Yet, it is important to note that the process of "Americanization" does not refer to a replication of American litigation proceedings. This is evidenced by the fact that, for example, American-style discovery has not gained the majority's approval among international arbitration practitioners.

The issue of "Americanization" has its roots in the distinction between Anglo-Saxon (common law) and continental (civil law) legal systems. Both legal systems have significant differences, especially when it comes to procedure. While international arbitrators are not bound by any legal tradition, whether they have a common law, civil law, Islamic or other background, they will inevitably be inspired by it when determining the procedure according to their discretion. Thus, different legal backgrounds and cultures may have significant impact also on the conduct of the proceedings in international arbitration.

A tribunal consisting of civil law lawyers, for example, will be more inclined to adopt the approach of a civil law judge. This means that the arbitrator might follow a more "inquisitorial" procedure in which it is primarily up to him or her to identify and address legal issues, seek evidence, and probe the factual record.

The aim of such an approach would be to gather all the facts in order to establish the truth. A common law arbitrator, on the other hand, might rather take on the role of a more passive referee, as is common for a common law judge. In this case, it would be primarily the parties, and especially their representatives, who are responsible for providing the facts and the evidence to the tribunal. Procedures such as broad, party-initiated discovery, depositions, lengthy oral hearings, and counsel-controlled direct and cross-examination are familiar to common law lawyers. This means that such procedures might also have an influence on the conduct of arbitral proceedings.

Moreover, briefs and hearings are of different importance and, therefore, handled differently in the two legal systems. In civil law countries, the parties' written submissions are of much greater importance than briefs in common law countries. As they are supposed to contain all pleadings of fact and law which a party wishes to invoke in the proceedings, they are very comprehensive ("frontloading"). At the same time, the hearings play only a limited role, as most of the statements have already been exchanged. In contrast, written briefs in common law jurisdictions primarily aim at launching the proceedings, not at frontloading all the pleadings of fact and law. Greater importance is attached to the oral hearings, which are scheduled accordingly.

International arbitrations usually follow a mixture of both legal systems: While the written phase has been largely adopted from the civil law systems, the oral phase is heavily influenced by common law characteristics.

8. THE SEAT OF ARBITRATION IS PARAMOUNT TO THE SUCCESS OF THE PROCEEDINGS, BUT HEARINGS CAN BE HELD ELSEWHERE

The seat of arbitration has significant legal implications and is therefore an important decision to be made in international arbitration. By referring to the seat of arbitration, reference is made to the jurisdiction (country) where an international arbitration has its legal domicile.

Such "legal" seat of arbitration must not be confused with the physical place of the arbitration. The physical place of arbitration merely refers to the city or country where the hearings of the arbitration are conducted. Seat and place of arbitration may diverge. If there are several hearings, there may also be several places of arbitration. While the first hearing may be held in Germany, for example, the second hearing may take place in France. Criteria for the choice of the place of arbitration are mainly of an economic and logistical nature. The location of the parties, the availability of adequate hearing rooms and the cost of such facilities are the most important considerations to be taken into account. Of course, aspects of travel can play a role as well. Oral hearings can be held at any place, as the place of arbitration usually has no legal implications for the proceedings. In some jurisdictions, however, it is mandatory that the oral hearings (at least one) be held at the legal seat of arbitration.

The situation is different with the seat of arbitration, the legal implications of which can be decisive. The seat of arbitration is an important connecting factor. First of all, it usually determines the *lex arbitri*, *i.e.* the arbitration statute of a country which is the legal framework for any arbitration proceeding. It provides rules for the conduct of the proceedings as well as for the form, notification and annulment of the award. If the arbitration statute of a country is applicable, the parties cannot exclude the statute's mandatory provisions. Any agreement by the parties has to be in line with the mandatory provisions, and the arbitrators must abide by them. Otherwise, they risk having the award set aside.

Therefore, it is important to consider the differences between possible arbitration statutes. While some statutes provide for detailed procedural rules, others are drawn in broad terms. Most importantly, there are significant differences with respect to their legal content, such as the arbitrability of disputes, the powers of arbitrators, and the availability of court assistance. Each state decides for itself whether or not to reserve certain types of disputes for resolution through its state courts (see II. 2). Thus, the arbitrability of a dispute may depend on the respective arbitration statute. To avoid surprises in the course of the proceedings, the parties should consider the powers of the arbitrators at the potential seats. The availability of efficient court assistance during the proceedings is also important. Assistance may be necessary, for example, if orders or interim measures need to be enforced by a court, as arbitral tribunals do not have the power to do so (see VII. 2). In addition to the legal aspects mentioned, arbitration statutes usually contain several other important procedural rules.

These legal considerations should be the basis for any decision concerning the seat of arbitration. However, there are other considerations. One key consideration is whether or not the seat selected is in a country that is a signatory to the New York Convention. This will be decisive when it comes to the enforcement of an award. Further, parties are well advised to opt for a seat which has proven to provide for a developed and adequate legal framework for arbitral proceedings.

Second, the seat defines the jurisdiction of national courts to review the award. A national court is competent to decide on a review of an arbitral award if the arbitration was seated in the country where the court is located. Jurisdiction cannot be transferred to a court in another country without transferring the seat of arbitration to that country. This is a classic scheme followed by most arbitration statutes. However, there are arbitration statutes that extend the jurisdiction of national courts to cases where the seat of arbitration is abroad. German arbitration law does this, for example, in Section 1062 (2) of the German Code of Civil Procedure.

9. OPENING STATEMENTS CAN MAKE A DIFFERENCE

Evidentiary hearings are a key element of most international arbitration proceedings. Their structure and conduct depend on the circumstances of the particular case, but above all on the discretion and preferences of the arbitral tribunal.

Nonetheless, it is possible to give an outline of the typical steps in a hearing. Usually, a hearing begins with introductory and organizational statements by the arbitral tribunal (especially the president). This may be followed by opening statements. After the opening statements, the tribunal proceeds with the examination of witnesses, and at the conclusion of the hearing, the parties' counsels usually hold their closing statements. The latter are frequently replaced by written post-hearing briefs.

Opening statement are presentations by the parties' counsel aimed at presenting the respective positions and cases at the outset of the hearing. They contain a mixture of substantive arguments and the existing and anticipated evidence. For the sake of comprehensibility, counsel will usually use audiovisual materials such as handouts (a "hearing bundle") or demonstrative evidence. In most cases, the claimant will start, and the respondent will be second. However, the order of presentations may depend on the respective case. If circumstances require (e. g. in the case of a counterclaim), the respondent may begin with its statement as well.

The duration of opening statements can vary significantly; it may range from 30 minutes to a day, or even take several days or weeks. It always depends on the complexity of the case, the arbitrators' instructions, and the respective counsel. Lawyers with a common law background often wish to make rather extensive opening statements. However, considering the necessary time limits, it is common practice in international arbitration to allocate only a limited time for the opening statement to each party. The limitation allows the arbitral tribunal to focus on the examination of witnesses. To provide clarity and support the efficiency of the hearing, the tribunal will usually explain to the parties in advance of the hearing the manner in which it will conduct the hearing.

Since parties are not obliged to hold opening statements, it is possible to waive this right. As a general rule, however, a party should not forgo such an opportunity. The reason is simple: first impressions are lasting. And opening statements are a perfect means to make a favorable first impression. They are the beginning of the arbitral hearing; therefore, the importance of an effective opening statement cannot be overstated. The aim is to persuade the arbitral tribunal at the outset of the hearing and to provide the tribunal with a roadmap for a decision in favor of one's own party. And with an opening statement and a well-compiled hearing bundle, the party can focus the tribunal's attention on the most important aspects of the party's position. The party also ensures that the tribunal is aware of the relevant arguments and the evidence.

A party should waive its opening statement only under extraordinary circumstances. One situation in which an opening statement could be a waste of time and money is when the other party fails to attend the hearing. Furthermore, an opening statement may be waived when the parties are faced with a case of low complexity and an arbitral tribunal that already has full knowledge of the submissions and evidence presented. In this case, opening statements may lead to unnecessary doublings that would be both annoying and boring for the arbitrators. Similarly, an opening statement may be superfluous where significant aspects of the legal argument are only possible after the examination of witnesses is completed. If factual evidence is decisive, a counsel should consider waiving his opening statement in order to focus on the crucial aspects of the dispute. However, this is a rare scenario.

10. CONFIDENTIALITY SHOULD NOT BE ASSUMED

One of the advantages of arbitration is often thought to be the principle of confidentiality. Parties might have chosen to settle their dispute before an arbitral tribunal, *inter alia*, in order to avoid emotive press releases or other damaging disclosures such as the publishing of commercially-sensitive information to their competitor.

However, most international arbitration legislation is silent on the subject of confidentiality of international arbitral processes. Indeed, there is no such principle of confidentiality that automatically applies to arbitration. If the parties have not contractually agreed on confidentiality, and if the statutory arbitration law at the seat of arbitration does not explicitly provide for confidentiality, it depends on whether an implied obligation of confidentiality is recognized. There are a number of jurisdictions in which national courts have cited a general, implied obligation of confidentiality for parties to international arbitration agreements, presumptively forbidding disclosure of any non-public materials submitted or produced in the arbitration to third parties (including the arbitral award). In other jurisdictions, courts have held that there is no implied or inherent duty of confidentiality on parties to international arbitration agreements, while also concluding that specific aspects of the arbitral process (e.g. hearings, arbitrator deliberations) are implicitly confidential. Nowadays there is a certain tendency to be less restrictive with the confidentiality of arbitral proceedings, and arbitration institutions have started publishing information on their proceedings (e.g. on which arbitrators are sitting in arbitrations etc.).

That is why it is advisable that the parties and the arbitral tribunal consider beforehand whether and to what extent confidentiality of the arbitration is desired. It is well-settled in virtually all developed legal systems that the parties' autonomy with regard to the confidentiality of international arbitral proceedings is to be recognized. Thus, the parties should work out an express confidentiality agreement when establishing the procedural rules of their arbitration process (if a confidentiality agreement has not already been included in the arbitration agreement). The parties should answer the following questions: (*i*) does the duty of confidentiality extend only to commercially sensitive information and awards or to all information relating to the proceedings? (*ii*) Are witnesses obligated to maintain confidentiality? If yes, how can this be ensured? (*iii*) Does confidentiality have to be maintained (to the extent possible) during court proceedings arising out of arbitration? Furthermore, parties should determine the confidentiality standards they wish to have applied to all documents exchanged, and they should lay down a code of practice to avoid unintended document disclosure. This ensures non-disclosure of business secrets. The parties might state that in the case of unintended disclosure, the defaulting party is held liable to compensate the other party. However, the parties should be aware that if confidential information is disclosed, the damage is done, and it is hardly possible to compensate for such damage.

One should keep in mind that a confidentiality agreement only binds the parties themselves, not third parties (including witnesses). In general, third parties are free to disclose materials from arbitral proceedings that have been provided to them without separate confidentiality restrictions. Also, third parties are generally free to seek compulsory disclosure of materials produced in or in connection with arbitral proceedings from the parties to those proceedings, without being restricted by confidentiality provisions agreed to by the parties. Hence, if desired, the parties should think of ways to ensure confidentiality of third parties. For example, statements, tribunal's deliberations and the final award could be maintained as confidential by the tribunal, parties, witnesses, experts and administrative personnel. The latter might be requested to sign a confidentiality undertaking.

"Confidentiality" in arbitration has to be distinguished from the term "privacy". Confidentiality comprises the obligation not to disclose information concerning the arbitration to third parties, e.g. a disclosure of hearing transcripts, written pleadings and submissions, evidence adduced, materials produced as well the arbitral award and orders. While confidentiality should not be assumed, the concept of privacy is an internationally accepted arbitration rule. The notion of privacy refers to the rule that only the parties – and not third parties – may attend arbitral hearings or otherwise participate in the arbitral proceedings. Privacy thus prevents any direct interference of third parties in the arbitration process and enables the parties to keep their arbitration process confidential. "Privacy" itself, however, does not necessarily require an arbitration process to be confidential. It might be difficult to determine what a "third party" is in order to decide whether the party may attend a hearing. Obviously, counsels to a party are not considered third parties. However, the issue may arise if representatives of an affiliate of the party to an arbitration want to attend a hearing. The arbitral tribunal must decide on a case-by-case basis if such a person is an unrelated third party or a representative of the party to the arbitration. The latter is the case if the in-house legal counsel is employed by the parent company in a centralized legal department but competent to handle disputes of all affiliated companies. In such a case, the person would be considered the representative of the party to the arbitration and would not be a third party.

V.

TAKING OF EVIDENCE

1. PARTIES AND TRIBUNALS OFTEN RELY ON THE IBA RULES ON THE TAKING OF EVIDENCE IN INTERNATIONAL ARBITRATION

Unlike in domestic litigation cases, there is no binding code of procedure determining the rules for the taking of evidence in international arbitration. Nor do the rules of the arbitration institutions make any reference to the matter. This is not an oversight. International arbitration brings together arbitration practitioners from all over the world with different legal backgrounds. Therefore, a one-size-fits-all set of procedures for the taking of evidence is not possible, and it is best to leave it to the parties and the tribunal to agree on the most suitable set of rules. Nevertheless, since certain customs and practices regarding the taking of evidence have evolved over the years, it seemed useful to "codify" these practices as a kind of soft law.

In 1999, the International Bar Association ("IBA") adopted the *Rules on the Taking of Evidence in International Commercial Arbitration*. These rules were revised and renamed into the *IBA Rules for the Taking of Evidence in International Arbitration* by the IBA Council on May 29, 2010 and updated on 17 December 2020 (http://tinyurl.com/iba-Arbitration-Guidelines) ("IBA Rules"). The stated goal of the IBA Rules is to be a

> "resource to parties and to arbitrators to provide an efficient, economical and fair process for the taking of evidence in international arbitration"

(see Foreword to the IBA Rules on the Taking of Evidence in International Commercial Arbitration). The rules include mechanisms for the presentation of documents, witnesses of fact, expert witnesses, as well as for the conduct of evidentiary hearings. As the rules themselves explain, they

> "reflect procedures in use in many different legal systems, and they may be particularly useful when the parties come from different legal cultures"

(Foreword to the IBA Rules).

The importance of the IBA Rules for the conduct of international arbitral proceedings today cannot be overstated. Even though they are not law, they are often used and referred to in arbitral proceedings. There are two ways in which the IBA Rules can take effect or become relevant.

First, the parties may explicitly include the IBA Rules by agreement. This can either be done in the arbitration agreement, or the parties can agree on the application of the IBA Rules *ad hoc* – at their own motion or upon the arbitrators' proposal – once a dispute has arisen. However, such agreements are rare in practice.

The second and more common method of including the IBA Rules is to permit the tribunal to refer to the Rules if it deems this appropriate. In this case, the procedural rules may include a statement along the following lines:

> The arbitral tribunal may [sometimes added: upon consultation with the parties] take guidance from the IBA Rules on The Taking of Evidence in International Arbitration when deciding on the procedure for the taking of evidence.

Strictly speaking, this is just a clarification. If no agreement is reached between the parties on how the evidence is to be taken, the applicable law and the institutional rules automatically leave it to the tribunal's discretion to determine the procedure. The tribunal could therefore take guidance from the IBA Rules even without explicit authorization.

While the IBA Rules were designed to bridge the gap between practitioners from different legal cultures, in particular common law and civil law, they do not quite represent the middle ground between the two cultures. In particular with respect to the method of examining fact witnesses, they lean on the common law tradition. Article 8 (4) of the IBA Rules is modelled around the common law tradition where questions are predominantly asked by the lawyers. It also provides for the typical three-step procedure of direct testimony, cross-examination, and re-examination.

The civil law influence can be seen in the strong position that the IBA Rules attribute to the arbitral tribunal. The prevailing principle laid down in Article 8 (3) of the IBA Rules is that the tribunal shall have complete control over the evidentiary hearing at all times. Article 8 (4) lit. g of the IBA Rules clarifies that the arbitrators may ask questions to the witnesses at any time. Accordingly, they may also "interrupt" the questioning by the lawyers. Further, the Rules state that the tribunal may limit or exclude any questions to the witnesses if it considers such questions irrelevant, immaterial, unreasonably burdensome, duplicative, or covered by the reasons set forth in Article 9 (2) of the IBA Rules.

Accordingly, it is fair to say that the civil law tradition is more reflected in the IBA Rules' provisions on the tribunal, while the common law tradition has influenced the role of the lawyer in the taking of evidence. Civil law lawyers acting as counsel therefore make the greater concession with regard to the method of witness questioning, and they are well advised to learn the ropes of the common law style examination. In today's practice, the Rules have their importance beyond a mere common denominator when there is a clash of legal cultures. Even when the parties to the dispute have the same legal background, the IBA Rules are often employed.

While an alternative, more civil law oriented set of rules was promulgated in form of the Prague Rules in 2018 (www.praguerules.com), it remains to be seen whether practitioners will accept these rules as an alternative to the IBA Rules.

2. DOCUMENT PRODUCTION CAN BE A BLESSING AND A CURSE

While differences between the common law and the civil law systems are being leveled in many respects, the taking of evidence is one area where such differences still exist. Both systems take a different stance on the parties' possibilities of obtaining documents which are in the other party's possession, including, or rather, especially harmful documents.

Many civil law jurisdictions follow the notion that each party must make do with the documents in its possession in order to make its case and discharge its burden of proof. The parties' possibilities of demanding documents in the other party's possession are typically very limited. Common law countries traditionally provide for so-called pre-trial discovery, i. e. a phase prior to the commencement of a trial that is designed to reveal facts and develop evidence.

Since there are no set procedural rules governing arbitral proceedings, each arbitration has to define its own approach to document production. In practice, there is a plethora of options, ranging from no document production at all to full-fledged and far-reaching discovery proceedings. As a general rule, the options for document production increase to the extent that there is a common law angle in the specific arbitration, whether due to the seat of the arbitration, the applicable law, or the nationality of the parties and the arbitrators.

In order to bridge the gap between the different systems, the IBA Rules attempt to provide some middle ground for document production. The gist of this approach is described in the official commentary to the IBA Rules as follows:

> "Expansive American- or English-style discovery is generally inappropriate in international arbitration. Rather, requests for documents to be produced should be carefully tailored to issues that are relevant and material to the determination of the case. … At the same time, however, it was believed that there is a general consensus, even among practitioners from civil law countries, that some level of document production is appropriate in international arbitration."

The IBA Rules' approach to document production is described in Article 3 of the IBA Rules. Accordingly, the parties can submit so-called requests to produce (Article 3 (2) of the IBA Rules) for individual documents or a "*narrow and specific … category of Documents*" (Article 3 (3) lit. a (ii) of the IBA Rules). The idea is to avoid fishing expeditions aimed at defining a case in the first place, rather than proving an already pleaded case. Nevertheless, the IBA Rules are very flexible, so that extensive document requests remain possible under their regime; whether such requests are then condoned or not depends mainly on the arbitral tribunal.

The costs of document production can be considerable, in particular in the case of requests for so-called e-discovery. Here, a party demands that the other side must conduct searches for electronic documents (email, etc.) using certain search terms. The possibility of such "e-discoveries" is mentioned in the IBA Rules (Article 3 (3) lit. a (ii) of the IBA Rules). While such e-discoveries are still rare in arbitration, the increasing number of electronically created and stored documents will also lead to more of them.

The costs of preparing such data, analyzing whether the data can be processed against the backdrop of data protection law, and then conducting the searches, can easily reach six-figure sums. At the same time, cases where document productions produce a "smoking gun" or other information that proves to be the lynchpin of the case are rare. Parties are therefore well advised to consider limiting the right to document production at the outset. The most extreme form would be to exclude document production in the arbitration agreement (see e.g. Art. 4.2 of the Prague Rules, encouraging the parties to avoid any form of document production). However, such an agreement, while valid, may turn out to be too rigid and prevent document production even in cases where it would be useful. As an alternative, the parties may include language in the arbitration agreement expressing that the parties wish the arbitral tribunal to follow a conservative or restrained approach to document production.

3. DOCUMENT PRODUCTION IN PRACTICE – THE REDFERN SCHEDULE

In most cases, the arbitration agreement will be silent with regard to document production. The tribunal and the parties therefore ought to discuss at an early stage, e.g. during a case management conference or an early procedural conference, whether and how document production shall occur.

If parties agree to have a separate phase in the procedural calendar for document production, such phase will frequently be provided for after the exchange of a first round of written submissions. Based on the information contained in these submissions, the parties can define the documents which they would like to obtain from the other side. Further, the tribunal can decide, if necessary, whether the requested documents are relevant and material to the case (see below). If a document production phase is carried out earlier, i.e. directly after the initiation of the arbitration, it is difficult for the arbitral tribunal to assess whether documents are material or relevant.

In practice, parties frequently rely on so-called Redfern schedules to organize and carry out the document production phase (named after the English arbitration lawyer Alan Redfern). The Redfern schedule is a table usually including four columns. Each party prepares such a table for documents it requests the other side to produce. The **first column** indicates the documents, or categories of documents, that the party wishes to obtain from the other side (e.g. "*All documents exchanged between Respondent and ABC in the time between August 1 and October 1, 2015 regarding the feasibility of the XYZ Project*").

In the **second column**, the party gives reasons for the particular application, i.e. why the documents are relevant to the case and material to its outcome ("*The documents are relevant in order to demonstrate that Respondent, contrary to the allegations in the Statement of Defense, questioned the feasibility of XYZ Project from the beginning*").

After the tables have been exchanged, the respective other side comments on the request in the third column. In this **third column**, the party can either accept to produce the document or explain why it does not believe to be obligated to produce the document. The most common objection to a production of documents is that the requested document is not relevant to the case or material to its outcome. Other objections include the argument that trade secrets and other confidential information would be revealed if the document was produced. Sometimes, a party may argue that the production of the requested documents would be unreasonably burdensome, taking into account the relation between the effort, time and costs that would go into the production of the documents and their relevance. Another objection can be that the described document or category of documents does not exist. Finally, typical objections are so-called privileges, in particular the attorney-client-privilege. Depending on the applicable law, the parties may therefore be entitled to refuse the production of documents that concern the communication between attorney and client. In international cases, the legal question as to whether such privilege exists can be difficult to answer. It can also lead to unfair results if one party, due to its nationality and the nationality of its lawyers, can raise objections based on privileges whereas the other side cannot. In most international cases, tribunals therefore follow a pragmatic approach and consider such attorney-client-communications as privileged irrespective of a deeper legal analysis of the underlying laws.

It is to be noted, however, that such privilege only concerns the communication between the party and external lawyers. According to a decision by the European Court of Justice (Case C 550/07), the attorney-client-privilege does not attach to communication with an attorney who holds a position of employment with a client.

In the **fourth column**, the tribunal finally presents its decision on the respective requests. After the tribunal has rendered its decisions, the parties are obligated to produce the documents ordered to be produced by the tribunal within a prescribed timeframe.

If a party fails to comply with an order to produce certain documents, there is usually no remedy to enforce the order. However, as provided for in Article 9 (6) of the IBA Rules, the tribunal may infer that such document would be adverse to the interest of the party who failed to produce the document.

4. DIRECT TESTIMONY IS OFTEN REPLACED BY WITNESS STATEMENTS

There is no one-size-fits-all set of procedures for the taking of witness evidence in international arbitration. In most cases, neither the arbitration agreement nor the institutional rules agreed upon by the parties prescribe a specific procedure for the taking of evidence. The participants, i. e. the parties, their counsel, and the arbitral tribunal will have to agree on the particular terms. The specifics of such an agreement will largely depend on the seat of arbitration, the legal background of the participants, and the applicable law. In a domestic arbitration in a civil law country, say Germany, this may lead to a procedure in which the witnesses are predominantly examined by the tribunal and not by the parties' counsel. If this is the case, no formal direct examinations, cross-examinations and re-direct examinations will take place. As stated above, it is very typical in international arbitration for counsel to take the lead in examining witnesses. Usually, such examinations follow the three-step procedure laid down in Article 8 (4) of the IBA Rules:

> "(a) the Claimant shall ordinarily first present the testimony of its witnesses; followed by the Respondent presenting the testimony of its witnesses;
>
> (b) following direct testimony, any other Party may question such witness, in an order to be determined by the Arbitral Tribunal. The Party who initially presented the witness shall subsequently have the opportunity to ask additional questions on the matters raised in the other Parties' questioning."

This approach is similar to the typical common law approach of direct examination, cross-examination and re-direct examination.

During direct examination, or examination-in-chief, the counsel of the party presenting the witness questions the witness. The mode of questioning is usually open, i. e. non-leading. Today, direct examination is an almost forgotten art. In most cases, oral direct examination is replaced by witness statements, i. e. written accounts of the testimony the witness wishes to give. If this is the case, the written witness statement simply stands as direct evidence, without the witness presenting his or her testimony during the hearing (or only very briefly for about 10 to 15 minutes). The witness' oral examination then begins directly with cross-examination. The drafting of comprehensive and understandable witness statements is therefore essential.

It is common practice and fully accepted that witness statements are drafted by lawyers. Such drafting, however, must be based on thorough witness interviews. This practice of having witness statements drafted by lawyers becomes objectionable only if the lawyer is no longer the transcriber of the testimony, but the author. Sometimes lawyers succumb to the temptation to turn the witness statement into an extension of the written pleadings. Usually, however, such hidden pleadings are recognized as such by the tribunal or fall on the feet of the drafting attorney during cross-examination.

Witness statements basically serve two purposes. First, they allow the proceedings to be streamlined and the limited hearing time to be used efficiently. The tribunal and the opposing party know long before the hearing what the content of the respective witness testimony will be. As a result, the parties and the tribunal can decide to what extent it is necessary to actually hear the witness in person in the evidentiary hearing. If the opposing party waives its right to question a witness, the witness will usually not be heard in person, which saves time and cost. As clarified by Article 4 (8) of the IBA Rules, it does not amount to an acceptance of the facts stated in the witness statement if a party waives its right to cross-examine the witness.

According to Article 4 (5) lit. b of the IBA Rules, a witness statement shall contain

> "a full and detailed description of the facts, and the source of the witness's information as to those facts, sufficient to serve as the witness's evidence in the matter in dispute".

Even if witness statements stand as direct evidence, the parties are sometimes permitted to conduct a brief direct examination. The scope of such examination sometimes proves to be controversial. Given the fact that the witness statement is to contain a full and detailed description of the facts, witnesses should not be allowed to "surprise" the tribunal and the other party during the short direct examination with new facts, i. e. facts not mentioned in the witness statement,. However, the distinction between a – permitted – "embellishment" of a fact mentioned in a witness statement and the introduction of new facts is sometimes difficult to make and then leads to procedural argument. At any rate, parties are well advised to include in the procedural rules provisions on the necessary content of witness statements and the scope of any direct examination.

5. CROSS-EXAMINATION IS THE STANDARD

Although not carved in stone, the presentation of witness evidence in most international arbitrations follows the pattern of direct examination, cross-examination, and re-examination. As explained above, direct evidence is most often presented in the form of a witness statement, i. e. a written account of the testimony the witness wishes to give. However, the lion's share of most evidentiary hearings is taken up by cross-examination.

Cross-examination is the examination of a witness by the opposing party's counsel. It is the corrective to the direct testimony. The common law system in which cross-examination evolved is based on the notion that truth is best established by strong representations of the case by the parties themselves. Direct examination allows a party to tell its version of the facts. Cross-examination is the opposing party's opportunity to show that this version is not accurate and not reliable.

Cross-examination is not intended to bring the witness to admit that his or her testimony was untruthful; this is an unrealistic goal and is achieved only in Hollywood courtroom dramas. Impeaching a witness works in a more subtle way. Cross-examination is also not designed to gather information that the examiner needs in order to win the case. Fact-finding must be completed long before the hearing phase begins. The facts on which the parties intend to rely are presented in their written submissions, in the documents submitted to the record, and in the parties' witness testimonies.

The main purpose of cross-examination is to weaken the persuasiveness of the witness' account of the facts, i. e. to impeach the witness. A skilled cross-examiner does so by demonstrating that the witness' testimony cannot be safely relied upon. The witness' testimony is one of the other party's puzzle pieces. During cross-examination, the examiner has a chance to show that the pieces do not fit as nicely into the picture as argued by the opponent. This is usually done by pointing out contradictions and inconsistencies between the witness' testimony and other information on the record. The witness is therefore first made to confirm his or her testimony and is then confronted with the inconsistent information, whether in the form of documents, submissions, or other witnesses' testimony. Besides this main purpose, cross-examination can also be instrumental in having part of one's own case confirmed by the other party's witnesses. In addition, cross-examination may – within certain limits – be used to elicit information from a witness.

One of the most widespread, purported cross-examination rules is that the cross-examiner should not ask questions to which he or she does not know the answer (or whose answer he or she cannot prove wrong if the witness gives an unexpected answer). The theory behind this rule is as follows: cross-examination is about controlling and impeaching the witness. Whenever the cross-examiner asks an open-ended question to which he or she does not know the answer, Pandora's Box is opened. It is an invitation to an open, narrative answer, and it gives the witness an opportunity to digress. In this situation, the cross-examiner deserves the answer he or she then gets.

However, exceptions to the rule must also be made in international arbitration. If the cross-examiner knows the relevant answer, it is most likely included in the written submissions and witness statements. Chances are therefore good that the arbitrators also know the answer. Unless the cross-examiner intends to bore or even antagonize the tribunal, he or she must be prepared to take a greater risk and do more than just rehash the facts and arguments from the submissions. He or she ought therefore to be prepared to ask questions to which he or she does not know the answers. But, of course, the risk must be a controlled one. The "no-questions-to-which-you-do-not-know-the-answer" rule must therefore be modified: ask only questions to which you know the answers or to which you are prepared to deal with all possible answers.

6. RE-EXAMINATION IS NOT ALWAYS ADVISABLE

After cross-examination, the party who nominated the witness typically has the right to re-examine the witness. Generally, the re-examiner should use open questions, or as the IBA Rules put it, questions that may not be "*unreasonably leading*" (Article 8 (3) of the IBA Rules). The purpose of re-examination is to clarify or explain matters that have come up in cross-examination. It is an opportunity for the re-examiner to repair any damage that may have been done by the cross-examination.

Re-examination is never mandatory, so it is up to the attorney to decide whether to conduct such a re-examination. There are two typical situations in which a re-examination may be necessary. First, the cross-examiner may have elicited an incomplete or misleading testimony from the witness. If this is the case, re-examination serves the purpose of completing or correcting the testimony. Second, the witness may have made a mistake, used an ambiguous expression, or given an answer that is open to misinterpretation. Re-examination serves the purpose of removing the ambiguity.

As a general rule, re-examination is limited to issues addressed during cross-examination. The rule stands to reason if one keeps the purpose of re-examination in mind, i.e. to clarify or rectify issues that arose during cross-examination. To put it negatively, re-examination is not intended as an opportunity for the attorney to introduce matters that were forgotten in the witness statement or during direct examination. However, in the absence of strict rules of evidence, arbitrators usually give some leeway to re-examinations that go beyond matters addressed in the cross-examination. This is especially true if witness statements stand as direct evidence. With most tribunals, even a weak link to the matters addressed in cross-examination will do. The boundaries between what it admissible in re-examination and what is not are thus fluid.

Often, re-examination is not necessary. The examiner must apply good judgement in deciding whether or not to re-examine. The two guiding principles for the attorney in deciding whether or not re-examination is necessary are the following:

> If it ain't broke, don't fix it.

If the cross-examiner has not succeeded in eliciting any damaging, misleading, or otherwise harmful information from the witness, there is no need to re-examine. Not only would such futile examination be a waste of hearing time; as said before, by conducting a re-examination, the examiner sends the signal that he or she is concerned about the matters revealed by the witness' cross-examination.

If you can do no good, do no harm.

Second, the examiner should not re-examine just because the opponent managed to elicit some disadvantageous points during cross-examination. Maybe the opponent was able to reveal some inconsistencies or put the facts testified by the witness in a different light. But before starting a re-examination, the examiner must assess whether he or she can repair the damage done. Sometimes there may be an inconsistency, and it may indeed be harmful, but there is nothing that can be done about it. The following golden rule applies here: "*If you can do no good, do no harm!*" Going over the damaging information again without correcting it or at least putting it into perspective only makes things worse. Rehashing the harmful information only makes it more memorable for the arbitrators.

Sometimes waiving re-examination can be the right thing to do, even if the cross-examination produced some unfavorable results that ought to be repaired. As a re-examiner, you never know how difficult it will be to remedy the harmful testimony given during cross-examination. In the case of simple slips of the tongue, this may be easy; but in other situations, things may be more complicated, e. g. because the witness may not even know that and how his or her testimony was damaging. In addition, the witness will no longer be as astute as he or she was during direct examination. The witness will be less attentive and less receptive to even well-meant questions. This difficulty of not knowing whether the witness is mentally prepared to fix the damage done during cross-examination may, by itself, be a valid reason to decide against re-examination.

7. FAMILIARIZING AND PREPARING THE WITNESS: THERE ARE ETHICAL AND LEGAL LIMITATIONS

Whether and to what extent counsel may prepare witnesses for their appearance in the evidentiary hearing is a controversial issue.

Before trying to analyze whether and to what extent witness preparation is admissible, one must first define the meaning of witness preparation. To state the obvious: witness preparation must never be used to teach a witness what to say or to distort or change the testimony in other ways.

What other – legitimate – purposes can witness preparation serve? First of all, a counsel may wish to prepare a witness in order to make the witness aware of the general process of witness examination. This is sometimes referred to as witness familiarization. Accordingly, the witness will be informed about the participants in the arbitration, about the persons who will ask him or her questions, the general timeframe, etc. Often, the witness is also provided with general guidelines, such as to only answer questions the witness fully understands, the right to refrain from speculations, or to carefully read through any documents handed to him or her before answering questions. Such familiarization, i. e. a preparation that is not related to the content of the testimony, is usually unproblematic.

More problematic is a form of preparation that touches on the "content", i. e. the subject matter of the testimony. Preparation in this regard may take various forms, ranging from an informal conversation between the lawyer and the witness about the testimony to a full-fledged mock examination in which the preparing lawyer assumes the role of the cross-examiner.

The question of whether such preparation is permissible can only be answered by looking at the law applicable to the specific arbitration, e. g. the law at the seat of the arbitration or the laws applicable to the acting attorneys. Most jurisdictions do not expressly address this issue. German law, for instance, does not deal with the issue of witness preparation. This may be due to the fact that such preparation is uncommon in civil litigation and is therefore not addressed in laws or by-laws; nevertheless, it is generally assumed that counsel may prepare witnesses content-wise, since there is no law or by-law preventing counsel from doing so. Other countries, such as England & Wales, take a stricter stance. While solicitors are not expressly prohibited from preparing witnesses either, the profession usually refrains from preparing witnesses in order to avoid any impression that solicitors may have attempted to influence witnesses.

Since national laws and professional by-laws are usually silent on the issue of witness preparation, it is useful to look at the rules and guidelines promulgated by the IBA. While these are not laws and therefore cannot override mandatory laws, they constitute what the arbitration community considers to be best practice in international arbitration. Looking at the IBA Rules on the Taking of Evidence in International Arbitration, Article 4 (3) of the IBA Rules provides as follows:

> "It shall not be improper for a Party, its officers, employees, legal advisors or other representatives to interview witnesses or potential witnesses and to discuss their prospective testimony with them."

The IBA Guidelines on Party Representation in International Arbitration address witness preparation in Guidelines 23 and 24. Guideline 23 states the obvious principle that

> "A Party Representative should not invite or encourage a Witness to give false evidence".

Guideline 24 then specifically addresses witness preparation:

> "A Party Representative may, consistent with the principle that the evidence given should reflect the Witness's own account of relevant facts, events or circumstances, or the Expert's own analysis or opinion, meet or interact with Witnesses and Experts in order to discuss and prepare their prospective testimony."

The Guidelines' commentary in regard of Guideline 24 expressly permits "*practice questions and answers*":

> "Further, a Party Representative may assist a Witness in preparing for their testimony in direct and cross-examination, including through practice questions and answers (Guideline 24). Thus preparation may include a review of the procedures through which testimony will be elicited and preparation of both direct testimony and cross-examination. Such contact should however not alter the genuineness of the Witness or Expert evidence, which should always reflect the Witness's own account of relevant facts, events or circumstance, or the Expert's own analysis or opinion."

8. GOLDEN RULES FOR THE WITNESS DURING CROSS-EXAMINATION

Being cross-examined is a first for most witnesses, and it is a stressful experience. In order to alleviate this burden on a witness, it often proves useful in practice to provide the witness with certain "etiquette rules". There is nothing objectionable about handing down such rules to the witness. Skilled cross-examiners prepare thoroughly for cross-examination, often weeks. As stated before, their mission is not to gather information, but to discredit the witness. It is therefore only fair to level the playing field and save the witness from becoming easy prey.

Always tell the truth: An obvious but most important "rule" for any witness is to always stick to the truth. Frequently, fact witnesses in an arbitration are linked to the parties, e. g. because they are employees. This can lead to situations where a witness is preoccupied with anticipating whether his or her answers are "good or bad" for the party. Witnesses therefore need to know that they are testifying as individuals, not as a party. Any liabilities for false testimony will therefore have to be met by them individually. What is more, experienced tribunals will see through a witness who is tip-toeing around to avoid harmful answers and attach less weight to their testimony.

Do not answer questions you do not fully understand: Witnesses should never reply to unclear questions. In a normal conversation, it is fine or even expected that a person is forthcoming and tries to answer a question even if it is not fully clear. There is no need to do so during cross-examination. If the witness does not understand the question, he or she must ask for clarification.

Always ask for the document: During cross-examination, the examiner invariably confronts the witness with documents (parts from a contract, letters, faxes, emails, etc.). Whenever asked a document-related question, the witness must make sure he or she knows the document that is being referred to, and not just believe that he or she knows what documents are being referenced. By doing so, the witness avoids making careless mistakes.

Do not volunteer information: The witness must only answer the question that was asked, not more and not less. Any additional information will make the cross-examiner's life unnecessarily easy. He or she can use the volunteered information as a foothold for further questions. What is more, any surplus information can give rise to inconsistencies with previous or following statements, and these inconsistencies are what the opposing counsel needs to discredit the testimony. It is therefore essential to limit the answer to what has been asked.

Avoid speculations: As opposed to expert witnesses, it is not the task of fact witnesses to speculate. If a fact witness does not know the answer, he or she should simply say so, and stop. The advice is easy to give and hard to follow. In cases of uncertainty, people have a tendency to explain. As Francis L. Wellman has written in his classic work on cross-examination: "*Many people seem to fear that an "don't know" answer will be attributed to ignorance on their part.*" (Francis L. Wellman, *The Art of Cross-Examination*, 41). Instead of saying "*I don't know*" or "*I can't remember*", people are inclined to explain and to speculate, not only in order to seem less ignorant, but also to be helpful. To a certain extent, a witness must learn that it is not his or her job to be forthcoming and helpful to the cross-examiner.

Do not argue with the cross-examiner: The exchange of hostilities and bickering between the cross-examiner and the witness should be avoided at all times. A good witness ignores hostilities from the cross-examiner, and vice versa. Any such collateral squabbling deflects from the fact-finding mission and is tiring for the tribunal. It also deprives the witness of the tribunal's natural pro-witness bias. Knowing that a cross-examination is a new and unpleasant experience for the witness, whereas it is daily business for the examiner, arbitrators usually give the witness some credit of trust and feel inclined to protect the witness from overly aggressive cross-examination. A witness who "pays back in kind" indicates that he or she intends to compete with the examiner on an equal footing and forgoes the tribunal's protection.

9. THERE ARE DIFFERENT WAYS OF PRODUCING EXPERT WITNESS EVIDENCE

Expert witnesses play a crucial role in a large number of arbitrations. An expert is a witness whose opinion is – by virtue of education, training, certification, skills or experience – accepted by the arbitral tribunal as that of a person with special knowledge in a certain field. For instance, an accountant may prepare an opinion on a purchase price adjustment in a post-M&A dispute. Or a scheduling expert may provide an opinion on the reasons for a delay in a construction project. Or – in arbitrations where members of the tribunal are unfamiliar with the applicable law – expert opinions on certain points of law may be produced. The less the arbitral tribunal can assess the relevant questions itself, the more important such opinions become for the outcome of the arbitration.

Two types of expert witnesses are to be distinguished with regard to the entity nominating the expert, namely party-appointed expert witnesses and tribunal-appointed expert witnesses.

Each party may produce expert opinions on certain aspects of its case. The expert responsible for such an opinion then becomes an expert witness who can be examined, in particular cross-examined, by the other party, just as a fact witness is cross-examined on his or her witness statement. However, as provided in Article 5 (2) lit. c of the IBA Rules, such an expert has to be independent from the party putting forward the expert witness in order to be treated as a genuine expert witness and not as a "regular" witness or party.

If a party decides to submit an opinion by an expert witness, the opposing party will often choose to respond by retaining its own independent expert. It is usually advisable that the parties discuss with the tribunal at an early point in time, e. g. during a case management conference, whether and how the parties intend to rely on expert witnesses. The participants can then agree on a suitable framework and timeline for the submission of such opinions.

If both sides rely on expert opinions concerning a certain issue, the tribunal will be confronted with two expert opinions on the same issue, supporting the claimant's and the respondent's case respectively. Depending on the complexity and the technicalities of the issue to be resolved, the tribunal may not feel fully equipped to evaluate the conflicting expert opinions based on its own knowledge and experience and decide on that basis. If this is the case, the tribunal may retain a tribunal-appointed expert in order to help the tribunal to properly evaluate the opinions of the party-appointed experts. It is generally accepted that arbitral tribunals may do so after consultation with the parties (see e.g. Article 25 (4) of the ICC Rules and Article 6 (1) of the IBA Rules).

Needless to say, such procedure significantly increases the costs of the arbitration. Not only do the parties incur costs in terms of fees for the two party-appointed experts, but also for the tribunal-appointed expert (fees which must be paid by the parties). In addition, the parties incur significant fees for their lawyers collaborating with or cross-examining the experts. In complex cases, millions in fees can go into the preparation and presentation of expert opinions and the examination of experts.

To avoid the time and costs going into party-appointed experts, parties may consider retaining only one expert chosen by the tribunal or jointly by the parties to analyze the relevant issues. This would resemble the approach typically taken in state court litigation in civil law jurisdictions where party experts have traditionally been used sparingly. In civil law jurisdictions, such as Germany, party-appointed experts are looked at with some suspicion by the courts because their testimony is usually regarded as partial. Parties therefore usually avoid using their own experts because the added value is minor and the costs are high. Undoubtedly, there are some disadvantages to consider. For example, parties have less access to, and thus less control over, the actions of a single, tribunal-appointed or jointly appointed expert. In complex and complicated cases, parties may therefore run the risk that the expert may not fully understand and appreciate a party's position and reasoning and, as a result, reach false conclusions. Such mistakes are difficult to rectify once the tribunal-appointed expert, or an expert jointly appointed by the parties, has filed his or her final report. In larger international arbitration cases, there is therefore a strong tendency to use party-appointed experts.

10. WITNESS CONFERENCING – EXPERT WITNESSES MIGHT FIND THEMSELVES IN THE HOT TUB

Witness conferencing is a type of examination in which witnesses from both parties who testify on the same subject matter are heard at the same time. While this approach can be used for all types of witnesses, it is particularly useful for expert witnesses.

Witness conferencing eliminates the weaknesses that come along with the disparity of knowledge between lawyers and expert witnesses. The examining lawyer is not an expert in the subject matter covered by the expert evidence. The examiner's special knowledge, whether factual or technical, is almost always acquired through hearsay. The lawyer learns the facts to be covered in the examination from the client only for the purposes of the proceedings. Such knowledge is usually only "island knowledge" within a larger field of expertise. The lawyer can therefore confront the witness on an indirect basis only. Even the most thorough preparation does not turn the lawyer into a genuine expert. The more complex the issues become, the less sure-footed the examiner will be. Once the examination gets to the core issues, the examiner often follows a script, asking questions on topics he or she does not fully master. It is then easy for the expert witness to present the lawyer with an answer that the lawyer cannot handle.

Thus, in conventional examinations, knowledge does not stand against knowledge, but knowledge stands against the examiner's advocacy skills. In witness conferencing, expert knowledge stands against expert knowledge. The confrontation is therefore direct.

Another inherent disadvantage of the traditional examination method is that it is static and makes comparison between the expert witnesses difficult; the traditional examination method consists of a statement of one party's witness and a separate counter-statement by the opponent's witness. Sometimes, there are rebuttal statements, but this is where the "dialogue" ends. In witness conferencing, the expert witnesses' statements are juxtaposed and, therefore, easier to compare. There is also a real opportunity for replies and discussions.

Direct confrontation between witnesses requires careful structuring and moderation. If the expert witnesses were permitted to enter into an unmoderated discussion, such a discussion would inevitably wander off track, becoming personal or even aggressive. Therefore, like any debate, witness conferencing requires a person who acts as a neutral moderator. The neutral must ask questions that allow the witnesses to fully develop their arguments. The moderator is also responsible for making sure that the witnesses' shares in the conference are allocated in a fair manner; in addition, the moderator must ensure that the witnesses do not digress. Since this task must be performed by a neutral, only the tribunal, specifically the chairperson, can assume this role. The issues that the tribunal defines for the examination may not necessarily be the same ones that the parties believe to be relevant and material. And given that the lawyers, together with their parties, have spent much more time preparing the case, they usually have a deeper understanding of the case than the members of the tribunal. Accordingly, there is also a risk that the arbitrators will keep the witness conferencing within the boundaries of their personal understanding of the case. This understanding may fall short of the crucial issues in dispute.

After all, witness conferencing is only an option if the parties and the tribunal agree that it would be beneficial. If witness conferencing is to take place, it is essential that the topics and the format be carefully agreed upon between the parties and the tribunal in a pre-hearing conference. In practice, the parties' skepticism about witness conferencing can be reduced by granting the right to a limited cross-examination in addition to witness conferencing.

VI.

PSYCHOLOGY IN INTERNATIONAL ARBITRATION

1. THE THREE SECRETS OF SUCCESS: ORGANIZATION, ORGANIZATION, ORGANIZATION

The story goes that a seasoned and successful arbitration practitioner was once asked the secret of his impressive track record. His answer: "It is quite easy if you observe the three ground rules: Be organized, be organized, be organized." The story illustrates how important proper project organization is when it comes to preparing for an arbitration.

An arbitration is a project, and, like any other project, deserves proper project organization. Assuming that the amount in dispute is EUR 10 million and that the company generally targets a profit margin of 10 % with its day-to-day business activities, the arbitration equals a project of EUR 100 million. Any "normal" project of EUR 100 million would now be staffed with a dedicated project team, an entire floor of an office building would be placed at its disposal, and an adequate budget would be allocated to the project. Unfortunately, an arbitration is rarely considered a "normal" project. Instead, top management believes that an (already overworked) in-house counsel can run the project alone (in addition to his or her other ongoing tasks, of course) and that the existing legal budget should suffice to cover all costs related to the arbitration. An arbitration proceeding organized and managed in such a way is doomed to failure. Proper project organization for arbitral proceedings requires the following elements:

First and foremost, a document management system must be implemented to organize all documents potentially relevant for the arbitration. Even in a standard arbitration, countless documents are produced; submissions often consist of numerous thick files. These submitted documents are only a fraction of the documents and emails that are actually reviewed and analyzed in the attempt to locate potentially crucial evidence. Without a professional, IT-based document management system allowing an electronic full text research for each document, in-house counsel and outside counsel alike quickly get lost. And costs skyrocket when expensive lawyers spend "billable" time trying to find "the meeting protocol where Fact A was discussed" instead of having the document displayed on the screen after some clicks on the keyboard.

Second, there should be an organization chart clearly identifying who is responsible for what in the context of the arbitration. In a construction arbitration, for example, such a chart may include the company's in-house counsel, the project manager, the contract & claim manager, and engineers to answer technical questions. On the law firm's side, the chart may identify the lead partner and the associates handling the case, always along with their main area of responsibility (e.g. "delay analysis", "damage calculation"). In addition, third parties may be included in the chart, such as technical experts. Such a chart allows for proper planning of the resources required to handle the arbitration. And it allows for a task allocation to keep costs under control. For example, it is generally much cheaper if information is retrieved by an in-house team compared with a search conducted by outside counsel. However, this can only work if the party allocates adequate internal human resources to the project.

Third, a large arbitration deserves a project plan that identifies the various tasks along with the timeframes available to complete those tasks. The project plan must be reviewed regularly to determine potential delays or bottlenecks requiring additional resources to keep the arbitration on track. The project plan can be combined with a reporting tool that shows which tasks were completed in the last week and which tasks are to be tackled in the next week. Such weekly "last week/next week reports" are a relatively simple tool, allowing in-house counsel to easily fulfill their own reporting obligations vis-à-vis the management and to monitor costs incurred in the context of the arbitration.

"Be organized, be organized, be organized" – this ground rule is to be remembered in any arbitration. Not every arbitration requires such elaborate project management as described above (although an arbitration without proper document management is almost unthinkable nowadays). However, not actively ensuring the organization of an arbitration project is certainly a costly mistake.

2. ARBITRATION IS A MARATHON, NOT A SPRINT COMPETITION

At the outset of a large dispute, parties are typically in a fighting mood. The claimant's team is convinced that gross injustice was inflicted on them and that it is now the time to make amends. In addition, an important prize can be won in a major arbitration, both in the form of money and prestige for of the party itself and in the form of career opportunities for the persons obtaining that victory. While the enthusiasm on the respondent's side may be a little less, it is still there. The respondent feels treated unfairly and is committed to defending its case to the bitter end; any compromise is out of the question. At the outset of the arbitration, all individuals involved are dedicated to the common cause and filled with energy. Cooperation between outside counsel and the client's team is pleasant and smooth. There is a kind of jingoistic euphoria or vibrant "rah-rah patriotism" in the air.

Then reality kicks in. Already the initial phases of the arbitration take longer than planned early procedural decisions by the arbitral tribunal are disappointing, and the opposing party submits a brief which is much longer and more detailed than expected. In-house counsel and other employees start to realize that arbitration is not a fun exercise, that a lot of work is required, and that a quick win is not guaranteed. Outside counsel continuously requests tons of input and information which is not easily retrieved. Countless meetings on various levels take place. Top management requests regular reports and complains about the lack of progress. To make things worse, the company's auditors question the validity of the claim or the accuracy of the reserve considered in the company's balance sheet. In addition, in-house counsel now receives monthly, rather high invoices from the chosen law firm, which require several adjustments to the initial budget and corresponding budget justifications vis-à-vis the management. Whilst arbitration was first perceived as a fascinating new experience, it now – in the eyes of those tasked with the arbitration and in particular in the eyes of the responsible legal department – turns into a burdensome endeavor. Suddenly, team members begin to think about whether a project other than the current arbitration would be more beneficial for their further career. The initial enthusiasm fades away and is replaced by strange ideas: What about delegating the entire arbitration to outside counsel? After all, it is their job to run the arbitration, isn't it?

In a nutshell: parties to an arbitration rarely have a realistic idea of what to expect in arbitration. The reason for this is that few companies and in-house counsel have ever experienced full-fledged arbitration. Hence, parties to an arbitration often make the same fatal mistake as newcomers to a marathon. They start too fast and completely underestimate the distance to be covered. In a marathon, this mistake results in complete exhaustion after 30 kilometers. This is the moment when the proverbial "man with the hammer" appears and puts an end to the race: Death by fatigue. In an arbitration, a similar effect occurs when the party's key individuals get tired of the proceedings and lose interest in the arbitration. They stop full co-operation with outside counsel and turn their attention to other projects. The dispute is now perceived as a burden rooted in the past, not as a profit-bearing project deserving full support. This attitude either results in a premature termination of the arbitration race by way of an unfavorable settlement or a sub-standard performance in the last and often crucial arbitration phase, because the team is longing for an end of the perceived plague instead of fighting for victory. In the end, the arbitration is lost.

To counter this development, in-house counsel must ensure a solid expectation management from the outset of the arbitration. Parties in general and all team members in particular must be aware that arbitration is a marathon, not a sprint competition. Some stamina is essential for finishing successfully. Sufficient means must be allocated to the project. To prevail in an arbitration requires a fully committed and stable team of in-house counsel, other employees and outside counsel. It is key that all team members are sufficiently incentivized over the full time span of the arbitration.

3. CHOOSING THE RIGHT COUNSEL – EXPERIENCE IN ARBITRATION MAKES THE DIFFERENCE

Few companies are regularly involved in arbitral proceedings, and even fewer have the desire to change that. Correspondingly, few in-house counsel have experience in dealing with arbitration. Unlike in many state court proceedings, representation by outside counsel is not mandatory. However, already due to the lack of relevant experience, in-house counsel would be ill-advised to represent their company themselves without the assistance of outside counsel. Hence, the first task of an in-house counsel is to choose the right law firm or lawyer to act as outside counsel. Many in-house counsel tend to instruct either the tried and tested law firm that is also charged with regularly advising the company, or the law firm which provided advice in the transaction now being the source of the dispute, e. g. the M&A deal which has now resulted in a post-M&A dispute. As a matter of course, both law firms would happily accept the assignment: Handling an international arbitration constitutes interesting work (also because it is a "new experience" for most lawyers), and it promises to generate a high number of billable hours. Both of these reasons are hardly acceptable to the in-house counsel in charge. Here is what in-house counsel should actually take into consideration when choosing an arbitration counsel:

The more quick-witted state that the term MAFIA no longer stands for a criminal organization, but for "Mutual Association For International Arbitration". This is wrong, of course, but the humorous remark contains a grain of truth. The international arbitration scene is a close-knit community. Its "members" know each other well from many proceedings and arbitral conferences. They regularly meet in different roles, i. e. sometimes as counsel to a party and sometimes as arbitrators. One might well criticize this, but it remains a fact. Therefore, it makes a lot of sense to appoint a counsel who moves with ease on the international arbitration scene. Such counsel will know whom to select as arbitrator for a given case. He or she will know what makes this arbitrator tick and will be able to anticipate better than any outsider which line of argument to pursue and which to ignore. In addition, a counsel who is known to and respected by the arbitral tribunal is likely to have a head start in terms of personal credibility. For these reasons, the personal reputation of an individual attorney counts more than the general reputation of the law firm that constantly represents the company – arbitration is still a highly personalized legal business. And first and foremost, an experienced counsel knows the dos and don’ts in the world of arbitration. Such knowledge will make life easier for the arbitrators, whereas a lack of such knowledge would irritate them. Hence, in-house counsel should always ask what level of experience, specifically related to arbitral proceedings, outside counsel brings to the table. Contrary to popular belief, arbitration is very different from state court litigation, and experience in the latter can never substitute for the necessary hands-on experience in handling arbitration matters.

Specific arbitration experience is also more important than legal expertise in the subject matter of the dispute or specific industry experience. A post-M&A arbitration should be handled by an arbitration lawyer, not by an M&A specialist. The arbitration lawyer can easily acquire technical knowledge or expertise in specific areas of law. He or she can then communicate with the members of the arbitral tribunal who, in all likelihood, are not experts in that particular area of law themselves. A good arbitration lawyer therefore acts as a kind of “translator” vis-à-vis the arbitral tribunal, explaining factual and legal matters in a way that is easily understood by the tribunal. On the other hand, even the most seasoned M&A lawyer will be unable to quickly learn and adopt the techniques to cross-examine a witness, deliver a compelling opening statement, or administer the complex document production phase in a major arbitration.

4. GUERILLA TACTICS IN INTERNATIONAL ARBITRATION: NOT ALL IS FAIR IN LOVE AND WAR

Not every party to an arbitration is interested in a speedy and efficient resolution of the dispute. The reasons for obstructive or even destructive attitudes can be manifold. A party might have realized that its chances of success are slim. This party might then deliberately protract the proceedings in the hope of wearing down the opposing party and thereby driving it into a settlement. Such a strategy often proves successful if the opposing party initially underestimated the duration and costs of the arbitration. The long duration and the parallel increase in costs then create pressure from management to "somehow settle the dispute". A change in management can have a similar effect if the new management is eager to settle the old dispute so that responsibility for the unfavorable settlement of the case can still be blamed on the predecessor. Other parties might embark on guerilla tactics because they lack the funds to pay for the proceedings or to satisfy the legitimate claim. In a third scenario, the party using guerilla tactics might simply be hoping for a lucky break, i.e. the proverbial black swan that changes the entire legal assessment of the case. Said black swan could be new case law, embargoes against the opposing party, the sudden unavailability of a key witness, or political pressure that forces a party into abandoning its claim.

Guerilla tactics are most often aimed at delaying the proceedings and/or increasing the costs of the proceedings. A typical approach is to challenge the impartiality of the arbitrators at the outset, then to question each and every procedural decision of the arbitral tribunal, followed by another challenge of the arbitrators for heaving dealt with a procedural request "*in an obviously biased manner*". Another tactic is to frequently request extensions of time and additional rounds of briefs due to alleged "new" facts presented by the other party. In this way, the arbitration is turned into a never-ending story. A third tactic is to appoint an arbitrator who is obviously biased or not fit for the job, e.g. because he or she does not actually read and speak the language of the arbitration. More sophisticated guerilla tactics attempt to overreach the other party by launching surprise attacks, such as introducing new and important documents at a very late stage of the proceedings in order to deprive the opposing party of the opportunity to comment or offer counter-evidence. Similarly, a party might question a witness about topics not previously introduced into the proceedings in the written witness statements.

The use of guerilla tactics comes at a price. The arbitral tribunal will not be amused if its workload is increased by countless procedural maneuvers. The loss of the tribunal's sympathy might somehow be reflected in the final award, and be that "only" by a negative ruling on costs, in which the arbitral tribunal can take into account a party's procedural behavior. Nevertheless, guerilla tactics are often successful because international arbitral proceedings, unlike state court proceedings, are not based on detailed procedural rules prescribed by a code of civil procedure which is additionally backed by authoritative case law from a country's supreme court. In addition, non-cooperative parties can hardly be sanctioned for their behavior. Unlike in state court proceedings, there is no default judgment. Many arbitral tribunals are therefore unsure of how to deal with obstructive behavior and suffer from what is nowadays called "due process paranoia". This term describes the tribunal's exaggerated fear that its arbitral award might later be vacated on the grounds that the arbitral tribunal violated a party's right to be heard by rejecting belated submissions or dismissing unjustified procedural requests.

In-house counsel are therefore well advised to prepare to defend against guerilla tactics. This is especially true if pre-arbitration negotiations were very hostile or there are other reasons to fear that the opposing party may be inclined to foul play. An adequate countermeasure is to appoint a seasoned arbitrator and to press for a decision-friendly president of the tribunal. In addition, urging the arbitral tribunal to adopt additional and detailed special procedural rules reduces the scope for later maneuvering and guerilla tactics. Such special procedural rules provide the arbitral tribunal with a solid basis for dealing with unreasonable or belated requests. Finally, as always, in-house counsel must ensure appropriate expectation management within their own organization so that guerilla tactics fail to create the desired nuisance value.

5. PRESENTATION IS KEY: HOW STRUCTURING SUBMISSIONS AND EVIDENCE CAN INFLUENCE THE TRIBUNAL

"You never get a second chance to make a first impression."

This bonmot holds true for written submissions that a party files with the arbitral tribunal. The first impression gained by the arbitral tribunal is not derived from the submission's content, it is derived from its outward appearance. Avoid small print, use a font size of at least 12 points and generous line spacing, and leave a margin on the page for notes – all of which makes reading a submission a more pleasant experience. And what the arbitrator reads easily and without effort is simply better appreciated, also content-wise. Numbering the paragraphs of a submission is standard practice nowadays, since it eases the reference to specific statements and arguments. As far as structure is concerned, a professional submission starts with an executive summary to allow the reader (= arbitrator) a quick orientation. A table of contents is a must, as is a meaningful list of exhibits. Many arbitrators like to receive the submission also as a so-called "bible", i.e. in DIN A5 pocket format to ease transportation and reading while traveling. Adhering to all of these guidelines is certainly not rocket science. However, corresponding mistakes easily lead to the subconscious (and therefore particularly dangerous!) conclusion that the unprofessional outward appearance of the submission speaks volumes about its content.

Nowadays, most arbitrators also keep their files electronically and therefore expect to receive a professionally structured electronic version of the submission. Accordingly, it pays to prepare a submission that is fully linked to all attached documents, be that documentary evidence or legal references. Such fully linked submissions allow the arbitrator to double-click on a reference in the submission, and then the referenced document miraculously opens on the screen. This technique increases the likelihood that the arbitrator will take note of the attached document rather than filing it away on a bookshelf. Sometimes, arbitrators also ask for a fully searchable document so that they can type in keywords as they search for information.

A seasoned arbitration counsel will invest a lot of diligence in the presentation of the arguments. The first challenge is to write in an understandable manner. The author of the text already knows and understands beforehand what he or she is going to write, so the author always considers the text crystal clear.

Understanding the content precedes writing it down. From the reader's (= arbitrator's) perspective, the sequence of understanding is reversed. When he or she begins to read the text of a submission, he or she has no idea yet what message the author wants to convey. Reading comes first, (hopefully) followed by proper understanding. Few authors realize that understanding their text is not a given. Several techniques can be employed to mitigate this problem. Here are just a few examples: Rule 1 is to use short sentences and follow the KISS rule: Keep It Short and Simple. Rule 2 is to start a sentence with the subject and the verb, because this is what a reader is intuitively looking for. Rule 3 is to choose a subject which is relevant and understandable to the reader, if possible a person. Since the human brain processes images much faster than language, it makes sense to include graphics and images wherever possible. Documentary evidence should not only be referred to and attached as an exhibit, it should be inserted into the brief itself as a screenshot rather than a simple citation. Seeing a crucial email, spelling errors included, creates a sense of authenticity and importance which no simple quotation (or even worse: indirect speech and reference) can match. Finally, enumerating arguments makes it easier for readers to follow. As a rule of thumb, readers prefer to read no more than three arguments in support of a certain position. When there are more arguments, the reader tends to perceive an argued position as "complex" rather than "clear". These and other techniques for comprehensible writing have been scientifically proven, but are rarely used in practice. Many lawyers focus too much on the content of the submission, forgetting the specific needs of the reader.

In-house counsel should therefore pay particular attention to the way in which the arguments are presented by the mandated arbitration counsel. In particular, in-house counsel can act as test readers, taking on the role of the arbitrators in order to double-check whether the arguments are presented in a convincing, easy to digest manner.

6. THE PSYCHOLOGY OF PERSUASION – A WINNING STRATEGY SHOULD CONSIDER HOW THE HUMAN BRAIN WORKS

Arbitration is a decision-making process. The arbitrators decide on the dispute. Counsel's task is to impact the arbitrators' decision-making process with the ultimate goal of having the arbitrators decide in favor of counsel's client. In an ideal world, the arbitrators apply clear-cut legal rules to the demonstrated facts and then decide based on logic alone. However, arbitrators are human beings.

Human beings often arrive at their decisions in an illogical manner. Nobel laureate Daniel Kahneman has extensively researched this topic and identified countless heuristics or biases in his bestselling book "*Thinking, Fast and Slow*". Heuristics are rules of thumb which the human brain intuitively applies to make quick decisions. Our brain thus avoids the trouble and effort of thinking a problem through completely. The implication for an arbitration is obvious: in order to enhance the chances to prevail, counsel must do more than simply present facts along with a convincing legal analysis. Counsel needs to employ psychological persuasion techniques.

Some say that the best argument is the sympathy of the arbitral tribunal. That sounds overly simplistic, but the assertion is backed by what psychologists have labeled "liking bias". People tend to believe people they like. It is therefore beneficial in arbitration proceedings if counsel is and remains on good terms with the arbitral tribunal. For this reason, a party may have a psychological advantage if it is represented by counsel who is known to the arbitral tribunal. And counsel should avoid antagonizing the arbitral tribunal by ignoring the unwritten rules of arbitration or demonstrating that he or she has little or no respective experience.

Psychologically, it is advantageous to take the claimant role. Claimant can tell the arbitral tribunal the first "story" about what has truly happened. If this story is convincing and initially accepted by the arbitral tribunal, there is a high probability that the arbitral tribunal will uphold its initial assessment throughout the proceedings, even after hearing counter-arguments. The psychological background of this effect is that our brain hates to change an opinion once it has been formed; our brain simply finds it too burdensome to reassess a situation. This phenomenon is called the "confirmation bias": once the brain has formed an opinion, it prefers to defend and maintain it. To this end, our brain is wired to automatically filter out any information that contradicts our initial view, a phenomenon called "avoidance of cognitive dissonance". The consequence of this intuitive thought pattern is that in-house counsel should consider to initiate the proceedings themselves when, as is often the case, both parties assert claims and counter-claims against each other.

The term "hindsight bias" describes the tendency of our brain to include the ultimate outcome of an action when judging that action. Thus, if a certain action of a person resulted in a damage and the question now arises as to whether or not the person was negligent, it is a proven psychological tactic to emphasize the detrimental consequence of that action. Our brain intuitively prefers a storyline that holds somebody responsible for the damage. The brain tends to reconstruct the fact pattern accordingly. A hindsight bias created in this way can be combined with an attempt to create an anchoring effect in the arbitral tribunal by somewhat overstating the disputed action as "not just negligent, but intentional". Anchored in the "intentional concept", our brain tends to conclude that the action was "at least negligent" – which may suffice to argue full responsibility on the part of respondent.

It is, of course, also an ethical question to decide which psychological tricks should be employed to get into the minds of the arbitrators. However, knowing and understanding these tricks is also a precondition for planning counter-measures in case these tricks are used by the opposing party. Then the need arises to de-bias the arbitral tribunal. In any case, these examples show how important it is to consider psychological effects in arbitral proceedings. Counsel simply needs to understand what makes arbitrators tick and ultimately reach a decision.

7. THE 30/70 RULE MAKES COMPLETE WINNING DIFFICULT

In theory, most arbitral disputes ultimately require an unambiguous decision by the arbitral tribunal: either the claimant is right or not. However, practice beats theory. And in practice, many, if not most, arbitral proceedings end somewhere between 30 and 70 % of the amount originally claimed. Here are the reasons for this widespread phenomenon:

First, parties have a psychological tendency to overvalue their chances to succeed in an arbitration. The more we invest in arguing our position, the more we believe that we are right and the other side is wrong. Good arguments that are put forward against our position are intuitively linked to the (disliked) opposing party that raised the argument. Then the argument is automatically devaluated. This phenomenon is called "reactive devaluation". It results in an overly optimistic assessment of the own legal position. The 30/70 rule is then only a corrective factor for this initial overvaluation.

Second, every arbitral tribunal has the objective of reaching a "fair" decision, whereby the decision perceived as "fair" is not necessarily the legally correct decision. The arbitrators' gut feeling may trump the logically correct adjudication of the dispute. Such subjective perception is particularly strong when two reputable companies are fighting against each other, which makes it somewhat unlikely in the eyes of the arbitrators that one honorable party is completely right while the other honorable party is completely wrong.

Third, in each arbitration the arbitral tribunal makes several decisions, for example whether the arbitration agreement is valid, whether the argued claim is warranted, and whether claimant has actually suffered the stated damages. If an arbitral tribunal now decides one issue in favor of one party and if this decision was a narrow one, such an arbitral tribunal might intuitively be inclined to somehow "compensate" the losing party for the first narrow decision by deciding the next narrow issue in its favor. The overall result may then again well be in the 30/70 % range.

Fourth, the arbitrators may disagree in the deliberation of the award, and not only if one arbitrator acts as a partisan arbitrator, i. e. as an arbitrator who clearly advocates the case of the party that appointed him. It is natural that even after a lot of arguing, the members of an arbitral tribunal may arrive at different views on certain factual and legal topics. One way of dealing with such a scenario is to take majority decisions and to communicate this openly to the parties. The other, often preferred way is to "compromise" within an arbitral tribunal, i. e. to seek an overall compromise solution which can be joined by every member of the arbitral tribunal without having to include a dissenting opinion in the final award. And again this "compromise" will result in a decision within the 30/70 % range. Fifth, it has become popular for arbitral tribunals to submit a settlement proposal to the parties as is permitted under the ICC Rules, for example, and even encouraged under the rules of the German arbitration institution DIS. Experience shows that whenever such a settlement proposal is made, it is within the 30/70 % range because such a proposal seems fair. And if such a settlement proposal is rejected, the arbitrators will have the tendency to confirm the rejected proposal by an award which is not too far away from what was proposed earlier.

The resulting 30 to 70 % phenomenon is a fact, and a seasoned in-house counsel takes this phenomenon into consideration. In order not to become a victim of the 30 to 70 % phenomenon, it is a good idea to appoint an arbitrator who is known for clear-cut and quantified decisions. It also makes sense to present the structure of the case to the arbitral tribunal by means of a decision tree with quantified risks. Such transparency reduces the likelihood of murky compromise decisions. For the claimant, it is a good idea to prepare thoroughly and to work hard to argue the highest possible amount of damages, anticipating that the ultimate amount will be reduced in accordance with the 30 to 70 % rule. The bottom line of these considerations is that – without regard to the particularities of a single case – it is not improbable that the final award will be in a 30 to 70 % range compared to the amount originally claimed.

8. CULTURE AFFECTS ARBITRAL PROCEEDINGS

An arbitration is called "international" if the parties to the dispute come from different countries and jurisdictions. This can easily lead to a legal "culture shock". The parties have different ideas and opinions about how the arbitral proceeding should unfold. The situation is even more difficult if the members of the tribunal also come from different jurisdictions. For example, a Chinese claimant may face a German respondent, and the three arbitrators may come from the United States, Spain, and Singapore. From an academic perspective, this is a fascinating scenario. From a party's perspective, the imminent clash of legal cultures poses various challenges that prudent in-house counsel must consider when proceeding with the arbitration.

Let us illustrate the clash of legal cultures with a few examples. An arbitrator with an Anglo-American legal education will have a tendency to act rather passively in the administration of the proceedings. He or she is used to having the parties' counsels take the lead, e. g. when interrogating witnesses. Since the US lawyer is used to extensive document discovery in a pre-trial phase, he or she will also be rather lenient in granting document requests in an arbitration. An arbitrator with a continental European background is familiar with proactive judges and will most likely mirror such an attitude when acting as an arbitrator, e. g. by examining the witnesses himself and by communicating an early assessment of crucial issues to the parties. On the other hand, document production is an almost unknown procedural feature in civil law countries, so the arbitrator will be restrictive in approving respective requests. For a civil law arbitrator, the old Roman law rule "*iura novit curia*" applies, i. e. the court knows the law, so that the law does not have to be explained, let alone proven. The US arbitrator, however, is used to a concept where the law must be proven, especially if the applicable law is a "foreign" law – "foreign" in this context means any law other than the one the arbitrator is used to applying in his home country. With regard to questions of substantive law, different legal concepts may also play a role. Chinese parties, for example, perceive a contract largely as the summary of the status quo at the time of contract execution. If circumstances change, the contract must be renegotiated and adjusted to the new circumstances. On the contrary, a German party or a German arbitrator will consider contractual provisions as the final risk allocation covering all developments emerging during the term of the contract. Changed circumstances fall within the risk sphere of a party and must be shouldered by that party alone. An adjustment of the contract requires truly exceptional circumstances.

Being aware of different legal cultures and their impact on the decision-making process is therefore the key to keep control over the proceeding. A seasoned counsel with experience in international arbitral proceedings anticipates the typical problems which arise in this context. It often makes sense to address these issues openly with the arbitral tribunal and discuss an appropriate approach, simply to avoid unpleasant surprises. It might then turn out that a party's subjective idea of an efficient and fair proceeding is not followed. For example, the arbitral tribunal may rule that an extensive document production is permitted and that the parties are requested to "prove" the law by submitting expert evidence. A German party will rarely welcome such a ruling. But at least it is now transparent what will happen, so that the party can adjust its procedural approach accordingly. Seasoned counsel also know that with regard to many "culturally diverse" issues in an arbitration, a kind of "international" standard has been adopted, which is often contained in soft law rules, such as the recommendations issued by the International Bar Association ("IBA"). Such soft law rules are meant as a compromise between different legal cultures, and it is relatively easy to convince an arbitral tribunal that these balanced compromise rules should be adopted in order to avoid a complete clash of legal cultures.

9. THERE EXIST RULES TO BE OBSERVED WHEN ARBITRATORS ARE TRYING TO FACILITATE SETTLEMENT

Quite a number of arbitrations end in a settlement. In-house counsel must anticipate settlement discussions to occur at some stage of the proceedings and prepare diligently for them. Here are some ground rules for dealing professionally with a settlement proposal from the arbitral tribunal.

Nowadays, many arbitral tribunals encourage a settlement of the dispute at some stage of the proceedings. In earlier times, there was much debate about whether arbitrators should be permitted to act as settlement facilitators. In the Anglo-American system, a settlement proposal by a judge is still a no-go. It is considered biased behavior that exposes the judge to a challenge based on his "obvious" lack of impartiality. This perception has long been transferred to arbitral proceedings. However, most arbitration rules today make clear that arbitral tribunals are entitled or even encouraged to foster settlement discussions between the parties. Nevertheless, a seasoned arbitral tribunal will clarify beforehand that any comments made by the arbitral tribunal on the factual or legal aspects of the dispute, including a settlement proposal based thereon, must not be used to challenge the arbitral tribunal for lack of impartiality. The tribunal will make sure that a respective confirmation is properly recorded in the minutes of the meeting/hearing protocol. In-house counsel should double-check that this precaution has been taken before any settlement proposals are made by the arbitral tribunal. Otherwise, a favorable proposal by the tribunal might be rejected abruptly by the opposing party and then misused as a pretext that "this arbitral tribunal is obviously biased so that the entire arbitration needs a fresh start".

The key question, of course, is how a party should position itself when asked by the arbitral tribunal whether the tribunal should explain its current assessment of the case and make a settlement proposal. Many arbitrators like to facilitate a settlement for two reasons. The first reason is that arbitrators often view settlement facilitation as their *nobile officium*, i. e. they consider reconciling opposing parties a nobler task than deciding the dispute. The second reason is a more egoistic one: some arbitrators simply want to avoid having to write a long and detailed award. For both reasons, a party must anticipate the question:

> "Would you like us to make a settlement proposal?".

However: never give an answer right away; ask for a break. The answer to this question is an important tactical decision that requires careful consideration with the team. Often, the arbitrators expect a "yes" to their kind offer, and it appears somewhat impolite or even hostile to decline the offer. However, it is always easier to say "no" at an early stage, and the early stage is before a settlement proposal is on the table. Once the arbitral tribunal has made a settlement proposal, it will probably "defend" the accuracy and adequacy of that proposal with quite some vigor. And if the proposal is rejected, the psychological confirmation bias will induce the arbitral tribunal to arrive at a final award which is quite similar to the rejected proposal, and be that only to justify that its settlement proposal was a realistic one. The decision to listen to a settlement proposal is thus of crucial importance, and it unfolds a dynamic which can hardly be controlled in the further course of the proceedings.

The decision whether to listen to a settlement proposal should be influenced by the following factors: First, the party should have a clear, reasoned opinion about the true value of its claim or defense position, ideally based on a procedural risk analysis. Second, the party should be reasonably sure that the arbitral tribunal has actually read the file and digested the factual and legal arguments before making the proposal. Otherwise, the risk is too high that the tribunal might simply want to get rid of the case quickly by means of an arbitrary proposal (which might be a good thing for a party that has a really weak case!). Third, the 30/70% phenomenon plays a role, making it likely that the proposal will fall somewhere in that range. The tribunal assumes that any proposal that falls outside this range will be rejected by the disappointed "losing" party. The tribunal might also subconsciously believe that a settlement in this range is somewhat more "balanced" and "fair" than, say, a 90/10% split. Thinking through these factors allows for a reasoned decision as to whether a party should accept the tribunal's offer to find a settlement or whether a party is better off firmly requesting a final award.

10. CALDERBANK OFFERS CAN ENCOURAGE SETTLEMENT

In-house counsel who aim at shortening the proceedings or limiting the cost exposure in an arbitration might consider the use of a so-called Calderbank offer. This technique is named after the English court decision in which this approach was first used and accepted, namely *Calderbank v. Calderbank* [1975] 3 AII ER 333 (EWCA). Originally, a Calderbank offer involved the following: Party A submits a settlement offer to Party B without disclosing it to the judge or the arbitral tribunal. The settlement offer is rejected. After the judge or the tribunal has decided on the merits, Party A discloses the rejected settlement offer to the judge and argues as follows:

> "On Date X, I offered a settlement amount of Y. According to the final decision now rendered by the judge, Party B will receive even less than the amount I offered as a settlement amount. Consequence: If Party B had accepted my settlement proposal, all subsequent costs would have been avoided. Accordingly, Party B should now bear all costs incurred after the date of my settlement proposal".

The beauty of this approach is two-fold. First, the arbitral tribunal is not influenced in its decision-making by having to consider a settlement proposal. A party willing to settle may worry – with some justification – that the arbitral tribunal might adjust its ultimate decision to a known settlement offer by concluding (incorrectly) that the party making the offer has somehow conceded that it is not quite in the right and/or to be content with less than argued in the arbitration. Such strategic concerns might discourage a party from making a reasonable offer. Second, a Calderbank offer causes the receiving party to seriously consider the offer because an unreasonable rejection could trigger adverse financial consequences. With this in mind, and to further encourage reasonable settlement negotiations, that party might counter the settlement proposal with its own Calderbank offer, which now puts pressure on the other party to consider a reasonable settlement. A race for the "most reasonable" settlement offer has started. In an ideal world, Calderbank offers provide a safe space for settlement discussions, discourage unreasonable negotiation ploys, and encourage meaningful and realistic proposals for amicable dispute resolution.

The problem with Calderbank offers is that they are not (yet) an established, let alone generally accepted, practice in arbitral proceedings. Accordingly, a party wishing to implement that technique must prepare carefully. The preferable way forward is to openly discuss this option with the opposing party. In theory, this is easy because using the technique creates a win-win situation with no real disadvantage to either party. In practice, convincing the other party to use a Calderbank proceeding is difficult simply because the approach is not yet widely known. The opposing party will fear being overreached by an unknown procedural maneuver and therefore say "no" out of intuition, not reason. To counter this intuitive reaction, it is helpful to support the proposal with a reference to a neutral, purely informational source, such as this book. If this does not work, a second alternative is to bring up this approach in a procedural conference with the arbitral tribunal. More and more arbitration rules encourage tribunals and parties to consider such measures at an early stage of the proceedings, cp. Article 24 of the ICC Rules. A seasoned arbitral tribunal will openly discuss the pros and cons with the parties and, if the technique is accepted, implement easy-to-follow rules. Typically, Calderbank offers are then to be labeled "For settlement purposes only – confidential, save as to costs" to prevent a party from disclosing the settlement offer received to the arbitral tribunal for strategic gain. A third, albeit quite risky, alternative is to simply send a Calderbank offer to the opposing party and explain the concept. In the final cost proceedings, an arbitral tribunal has discretion to consider an unreasonable rejection of a Calderbank offer, e.g. under Article 38 (5) of the ICC Rules. Frankly, few arbitral tribunals will do so without some basis in the procedural rules or in the parties' agreement. What remains is the hope that the mere possibility of adverse consequences might encourage a party to seriously consider the submitted offer.

VII.

INTERIM MEASURES AND OTHER INTERACTIONS BETWEEN COURTS AND THE ARBITRAL TRIBUNAL

1. ARBITRAL TRIBUNALS HAVE JURISDICTION TO DECIDE ON INTERIM MEASURES DURING THE PROCEEDINGS

Arbitral proceedings can take a long time, and some issues simply cannot wait for the resolution of the entire dispute. To give just a few examples from practice: (1) A mining company learns that its former CEO is about to take a job with a competitor despite a non-compete agreement. (2) A construction company building an oil rig finds itself desperately short of cash because the employer withholds payments of some hundred million Euros. (3) A ship owner has a claim for outstanding charter fees, but the charterer is emptying his bank accounts and moving the money elsewhere.

In each of these examples (and countless others), irreparable damage may be done to a party that has to wait for the final decision in an international arbitration. This is where interim measures come into play. Sometimes they are indispensable. But even when they are not, they may still be a very tempting option: first, to put pressure on the opposing party; second, to achieve some success ahead of the final award – and as a source of good news to report to senior management.

In most jurisdictions, national arbitration laws allow arbitral tribunals to issue interim measures, if the parties have agreed to this. Article 17 (1) of the Model Law provides that

> "[u]nless otherwise agreed by the parties, the arbitral tribunal may, at the request of a party, grant interim measures".

National arbitration laws that bar tribunals from providing interim relief would arguably clash with the spirit (if not the letter) of the New York Convention.

As mentioned in the Model Law, it is usually assumed (i. e. absent agreements to the contrary) that the parties at least implicitly consented when concluding the arbitration agreement. In many cases, the parties will consent by selecting a set of arbitration rules that explicitly authorizes the tribunal to issue interim measures (*cf.* Article 25 of the LCIA Rules).

When dealing with a request for interim measures, tribunals will – generally speaking – ask the same or similar questions as state courts. They will ask what harm the applicant would suffer if the request was denied, and will weigh that against the harm that the opposing party would suffer if the request was granted.

Tribunals will then assess the urgency of the matter, i. e. whether the applicant has a reason to obtain the desired relief now rather than with the final award.

Finally, some tribunals will require the applicant to establish at least a *prima facie* case on jurisdiction and on the merits. This is a somewhat sensitive issue, as tribunals must be wary not to prejudge the merits of the entire case. However, by requiring a *prima facie* case, tribunals can establish a reasonable threshold which deters parties from flooding the tribunals with unjustified requests for interim measures. Similarly, the tribunal may require the applicant to provide security for potential damages that the opposing party may incur as a result of the interim measure. This, too, will motivate the applicant to file only "serious" requests.

In any event, parties should beware of being too trigger-happy with their requests for interim measures: under Article 17G of the Model Law, the applicant may be held liable for costs and damages if the measures are granted, but later turn out to be unjustified. Because of this clause (which was modeled on German arbitration law), an unjustified request for interim measures can have dramatic consequences, for example when a party is enjoined from entering into a lucrative contract. Therefore, before applying for interim relief, parties should check whether the respective jurisdiction has stipulations along the lines of Article 17G of the Model Law, and they should carefully consider what commercial implications the requested interim measures may have for the addressee.

2. ENFORCEABILITY OF INTERIM MEASURES ORDERED BY AN ARBITRAL TRIBUNAL DEPENDS ON DOMESTIC PROCEDURAL LAW

Arbitral tribunals may or may not order interim measures, but at any rate they cannot *enforce* interim measures. Arbitral tribunals cannot, on their own, seize a party's assets, freeze bank accounts, or have a party or its CEO arrested. At the end of the day, arbitral tribunals are private dispute resolution bodies and have no right to a share in the state's monopoly on the use of force (which is the ultimate sanction behind any kind of enforcement). For enforcement, therefore, the tribunal's decision must first be recognized and declared enforceable by national courts.

This begs the question: Do national courts have to comply with a request to enforce a tribunal's order for interim relief? If not, interim measures by arbitral tribunals have little legal clout.

For final awards, recognition is facilitated (and indeed required) by the New York Convention (see VIII.), but for interim awards, the situation is much less clear. A substantial body of case law and scholarly works opine that the New York Convention does not cover the recognition and enforcement of interim awards either way, i. e. neither requires nor prohibits their recognition and enforcement. Similarly, the Swiss Federal Tribunal has held that a preliminary award is not a final award and therefore cannot be set aside individually. By the same reasoning, such an award could be denied recognition and enforcement.

Fortunately, the question will quite often be moot. If an interim award does *not* qualify as an award within the meaning of the New York Convention, it can nevertheless be recognized and enforced in a specific jurisdiction if the applicable domestic procedural law so permits. A first indication of this can be obtained by checking whether and to what extent the respective jurisdiction has adopted the Model Law. The Model Law, in its most recent iteration, provides a model clause for the recognition of interim awards (Article 17H of the Model Law), along with a model clause stipulating some additional grounds on which recognition can be denied, as compared to the recognition of a final award (Article 17I of the Model Law). The Model Law is therefore a major step forward for all parties seeking interim relief in arbitration proceedings.

Even if the respective jurisdiction has not adopted the provisions of the Model Law, it may still provide statutory law or case law to the effect that interim awards can be recognized and enforced. This is the case in the US, for example. While the Federal Arbitration Act neither implements the Model Law nor takes a clear stance on interim relief, a number of US court decisions have ruled in favor of enforceability. For example, one US court has held that a decision labeled "interim order for security" constitutes a final award.

Therefore, whether by virtue of the Model Law or by virtue of some other law, interim awards issued by arbitral tribunals are enforceable in many jurisdictions. However, even if the applicable law does not permit recognition and enforcement, parties are well advised to consider whether they should not voluntarily comply with the tribunal's orders. Disobeying a tribunal's order will rarely endear a party to the tribunal, and may reduce this party's chances of prevailing on the main merits. And unlike an interim award, a final award on the merits benefits from the New York Convention when it comes to enforcement.

3. ARBITRATION DOES NOT BAR RECOURSE TO COURTS FOR INTERIM MEASURES

Although the road to interim relief from arbitral tribunals is thus clear, parties may still find themselves in a situation where they prefer, or even have to, apply to the state courts for interim relief directly, i. e. without first approaching the arbitral tribunal. There are several situations in which this might be the case. First, a party may request interim relief before the tribunal is constituted. Sometimes the party has the option to submit the matter to an emergency arbitrator (e. g. according to Article 29 of the ICC Rules – see III. 10), but not always.

Second, the matter may be so urgent that the party cannot wait until the two-step procedure explained above is completed, but must immediately turn to the state courts. And third, a party may feel that the tribunal – especially if the arbitrators have no legal training – lacks the legal expertise to navigate the minefield of interim relief.

Arguing against these considerations is the fact that the parties have concluded an arbitration agreement, which the opposing party could refer to in order to bring down a request for interim relief filed with the state courts. Indeed, some courts have held that the New York Convention – specifically Article II (3) of the New York Convention – prohibits the involvement of state courts through interim measures in pre-award arbitral proceedings. However, most jurisdictions now allow concurrent competence of arbitral tribunals and courts when it comes to interim measures. The Model Law, in particular, provides that despite the arbitration agreement, a party may request and a state court may grant interim measures "*before or during arbitral proceedings*" (Article 9 of the Model Law). Article 17J of the Model Law clarifies that the court shall have the same power "*as it has in relation to proceedings in courts*". Barring exceptional circumstances, such a request does not constitute a waiver of the right to invoke the arbitration clause.

That is not to say that the parties are entirely at liberty to apply to state courts, as if there was no arbitration agreement at all. Rather, many national laws will stipulate additional requirements for doing so. The Model Law, somewhat cautiously, tells state courts to

> "exercise such power (...) in consideration of the specific features of international arbitration".

The UK Arbitration Act 1996 is less reserved, telling courts that they

> "shall act only if or to the extent that the arbitral tribunal (...) has no power or is unable for the time being to act effectively"

(Article 44 (5) of the UK Arbitration Act 1996).

In addition, some arbitration rules restrict the parties' options to apply to state courts for interim relief by stipulating additional requirements. For example, Article 28 (2) of the ICC Rules tells the parties that they may approach the state courts for interim relief (*scil.:* only)

> "before the file is transmitted to the arbitral tribunal, and in appropriate circumstances thereafter".

Such restrictions raise the question of whether the parties could even go a step further and agree to prohibit state court involvement altogether. However, as agreements to this effect might exclude a party from effective legal recourse in specific circumstances, they may be considered to be against public policy and thus void. This is arguably the case in Germany.

As a result of the foregoing, parties will often be able to choose between state courts and arbitration as the forum in which to apply for interim relief. This raises the question of whether an arbitral tribunal can overturn a state court decision concerning interim relief – not by a final award on the merits (this is a given), but by an interim award and upon request of the party that lost in the state courts. Case law and scholarly works are divided on this subject, with answers ranging from "never!" to "always!", and everything in between. The bottom line is that legal practitioners faced with a request for interim relief in state courts are well advised not to rely on the arbitral tribunal to later overturn the court's decision; instead, the request should already be opposed with force in court.

4. ANTI-ARBITRATION INJUNCTIONS ARE RARE – BUT SOME JURISDICTIONS STILL ALLOW THEM

Anti-arbitration injunctions are orders issued by state courts or – in rare cases – arbitral tribunals. Through an anti-arbitration injunction, a party can theoretically compel (i) the opposing party not to commence arbitration proceedings, (ii) any of the parties and/or the arbitrators to stay the arbitral proceedings, or (iii) the opposing party not to pursue recognition and enforcement of the award.

Usually, parties who seek injunctive relief along these lines will argue that the arbitral tribunal in the targeted arbitration does not have jurisdiction and that they will suffer irreparable harm unless the opposing parties or the arbitrators are enjoined from proceeding.

The ICC has estimated that a mere 1 % of the registered arbitrations involved an anti-arbitration injunction (*J. D. M. Lew*, in: E. Gaillard, Anti-Suit Injunctions in International Arbitration, 2005, p. 33). At first glance, this number seems surprisingly low. After all, anti-arbitration injunctions serve legitimate interests: defending against an arbitration requires time and effort, even if the claim is ultimately dismissed for lack of jurisdiction; this is especially the case if a "frivolous" arbitration is brought in some remote corner of the globe. In addition, there is always the risk (however small) that an overeager tribunal decides that it has jurisdiction, and proceeds to judge the case on the merits. All trouble associated with this could be avoided by an anti-arbitration injunction issued in a party's home jurisdiction. And, of course, anti-arbitration injunctions could be imagined to be quite popular among less scrupulous parties as a way to impede access to justice.

Nevertheless, anti-arbitration injunctions are rare, and mainly for two reasons. First, in several popular arbitration venues, state courts do not issue anti-arbitration injunctions at all, nor do they recognize foreign ones. The reasoning behind this stance is that anti-arbitration injunctions can be considered incompatible with the cornerstones of international arbitration. For example, enjoining a party from commencing arbitral proceedings can be seen as contrary to the concept of competence-competence (see I. 1), because the arbitrators are denied the opportunity to rule on their own jurisdiction. As another example, enjoining a party from enforcing an award can be seen as contrary to the idea of general recognition of international awards, as spelled out in Article III of the New York Convention.

As a rule of thumb, civil law jurisdictions (e.g. Switzerland and Germany) have a less favorable view of anti-arbitration injunctions than common law jurisdictions (e.g. the United Kingdom and the United States). Accordingly, courts in civil law jurisdictions are less likely to issue or recognize anti-arbitration injunctions (although exceptions do exist). However, even among common law jurisdictions, some allow anti-arbitration injunctions only under exceptional circumstances or not at all, unless the arbitration is seated in that jurisdiction.

Second, and related: even if a party manages to obtain an anti-arbitration injunction in some jurisdiction, the addressees (opposing parties and/or arbitrators) may decide to go on with the arbitration anyway. They may do so because they deem such injunctions generally invalid, or because they do not feel bound by that particular injunction. They may also do so because they do not fear sanctions associated with their going against the injunction, e.g. because they feel safe in their own jurisdiction. Arbitrators, in particular, will have to assess carefully whether they should really heed an anti-arbitration injunction directed against them: halting the arbitral proceedings may well amount to a denial of justice and even constitute a breach of their contract with the parties who mandated them.

On the other hand, some of the jurisdictions that do permit anti-arbitration injunctions also impose severe fines for disregarding them. Arbitrators, in particular, will therefore be caught between the proverbial rock and the hard place, especially if they come from the jurisdiction where the injunction was issued. For all these reasons, anti-arbitration injunctions – however rare they may be in practice – are among the topics that should be carefully considered when choosing the seat of arbitration. In particular, in-house counsel should carefully consider the associated pitfalls before resorting by default to having the seat in a jurisdiction that permits anti-arbitration injunctions.

5. ANTI-SUIT INJUNCTIONS ARE INCREASINGLY RECOGNIZED IN SEVERAL JURISDICTIONS

In some cases, a party does not want an arbitration to commence or to go on; in other cases, it does not want a state court proceeding to commence or to go on. In the latter case, the party can attempt to obtain an anti-suit injunction. The party may seek to obtain such an injunction either from a state court or, if the arbitration has already begun, from the arbitral tribunal. In either case, the party will argue that the opposing party, by taking the matter to a state court, is in breach of the arbitration agreement.

Anti-suit injunctions have been discussed extensively in legal literature and case law. However, much of this discussion deals with situations in which the party applying for the injunction wants the dispute resolved not through arbitration, but in a specific state court which the parties had earlier agreed on. In other words, the anti-suit injunction is supposed to protect a choice-of-forum clause, not an arbitration agreement. In such situations, the main purpose of the anti-suit injunction is to prevent the opposing party from bringing "torpedo actions", i. e. lawsuits in a notoriously inefficient forum whose sole purpose is to prevent lawsuits in the proper forum.

"Torpedo actions" are particularly destructive to choice-of-forum clauses because the court in the proper forum may feel compelled to wait for the "torpedo action" to be resolved – either because of considerations of *lis pendens* or because of considerations of comity. If the parties have an arbitration agreement, torpedo actions are of limited use, and therefore the need for anti-suit injunctions is less pronounced. After all, arbitrators can usually rely on the principle of competence-competence and rule on their jurisdiction even if a competing action is still pending in the state courts (*cf.* Article 8 (2) of the Model Law). In addition, arbitrators will feel less (if at all) restricted by comity considerations than state courts. Nevertheless, apart from the residual legal uncertainty associated with a parallel state court proceeding, such a proceeding will at least cost time and money. Therefore, an injunction may be warranted.

In the European Union, anti-suit injunctions that aim at protecting mere choice-of-forum clauses are not permitted. However, anti-suit injunctions are permitted insofar as they aim at protecting arbitration agreements. And if an arbitral tribunal issues an award to that effect, then said award can be recognized and enforced in EU member states without violating EU law.

Permitted, however, does not mean *available*. In fact, anti-suit injunctions by state courts are available as a remedy only in some legal systems. In many others, state courts will not issue anti-suit injunctions, either to protect choice-of-forum clauses or to protect arbitration clauses.

However, arbitral tribunals will often consider themselves authorized to issue such injunctions, i. e. an award prohibiting a party from commencing (or continuing) a state court proceeding dealing with subject matters that the arbitration clause places in the hands of the tribunal. An arbitral tribunal may do so even if state courts at the seat of arbitration do not have such power. For example, Swiss courts are arguably not allowed to issue anti-suit injunctions, yet arbitral tribunals seated in Switzerland have done so on several occasions. Arbitral tribunals may do so because their power to issue injunctions comes not from statutory law, but from the arbitration agreement, if said agreement allows them to issue interim measures (e. g. Article 28 (1) of the ICC Rules).

Unlike anti-arbitration injunctions, anti-suit injunctions can reasonably enjoin only the opposing party from proceeding (and not the foreign courts). Therefore, their effectiveness depends on the opposing party being subject to the jurisdiction and to the sanctions imposed by the court that issues the injunction. An injunction issued by an arbitral tribunal must first be recognized before any sanctions can take hold. If the injunction is issued by way of an interlocutory award, recognition may not even be possible in some jurisdictions (see VII. 2). Of course, as with any other injunction issued by an arbitral tribunal, any party should think twice before disobeying it, even if the party has technically nothing to fear as a matter of law.

6. SOME JURISDICTIONS ALLOW FOR COURT REVIEW OF THE VALIDITY OF THE ARBITRATION AGREEMENT PRIOR TO COMMENCEMENT OF PROCEEDINGS

State courts frequently review the validity of arbitration agreements after the arbitral proceedings have been completed, as the invalidity of the agreement is one of the few grounds for refusing recognition and enforcement of an arbitral award under the New York Convention. Until that point, it is upon the arbitrators to decide whether the agreement is valid – and, as a general rule, *only* upon the arbitrators. This follows from the principle of competence-competence, i.e. the notion that the arbitrators themselves have the power to determine, on a preliminary basis, whether they are authorized to decide the case at hand.

While generally sound, this principle has its downsides in cases where the arbitration agreement is poorly drafted so that its validity is doubtful. In such cases, a party seeking legal recourse has two options, neither of which is particularly attractive. The party can take the matter to court – but the opposing party may then argue that the arbitration agreement is valid. Or the party can take the matter to arbitration – but the opposing party may then argue that the arbitration agreement is invalid. Arbitration will often be the safer bet because many jurisdictions these days take an arbitration-friendly stance, but there are arbitration agreements that are drafted so shoddily that the outcome is still unpredictable. In any case, the claimant runs the risk that its claim is dismissed on procedural grounds because the opposing party takes advantage of the poor drafting of the clause. Then the first lawsuit is nothing but a waste of time and money.

To address such situations, some jurisdictions deviate to some extent from the aforementioned principle, and provide parties the opportunity to have their agreement reviewed by a court before the arbitration even commences. In other words, the party seeking legal recourse can obtain a binding decision from the state courts as to whether or not the arbitration agreement is valid.

These jurisdictions do not have a uniform approach to court review, and the Model Law does not provide a blueprint. One of the more drastic approaches can be found in German law, under which parties – until the tribunal is constituted –

may file a request with the court to determine the admissibility or inadmissibility of arbitral proceedings (Section 1032 (2) of the German Code of Civil Procedure). The court's findings are then binding, so that in a next step, each party can commence proceedings before the state courts or an arbitral tribunal (as the case may be) without having to fear that its claim will be dismissed on this particular procedural issue.

This court review provides significant advantages, not least because the party's application is not a full-fledged claim; the review is therefore both faster and cheaper. However, as with any statutory solution to a complex legal problem, this court review may cause its own issues. One issue is that the review may "freeze" or at least slow down an arbitration that has been initiated while the review is still ongoing. German law explicitly allows the arbitral tribunal to proceed with the arbitration while the review is pending, and even to issue an award. In practice, however, arbitrators may nevertheless hesitate to do so and prefer to wait until the review is completed, rather than being told in the middle of a complicated proceeding that they do not have jurisdiction after all.

The up- and downsides of the court review have been discussed at length by legal scholars. For legal practitioners like in-house counsels, the point is largely moot, as the court review is either available at the chosen seat of arbitration or it is not. Instead, the main takeaway is twofold: (1) If the arbitration agreement is of questionable validity, the court review can be a cheap and quick way to obtain clarity. (2) The court review does not resolve all the issues associated with poorly drafted arbitration agreements, and therefore is no excuse for not paying attention in the drafting phase.

7. STATE COURTS HAVE AN IMPORTANT SAY IN CHALLENGE PROCEEDINGS

Interim measures are not the only occasion on which a party to an arbitration may seek the assistance of state courts. Two other important examples are challenges regarding jurisdiction (see IV. 5) and challenges against arbitrators (see III. 6).

With respect to the former, the parties to an arbitration sometimes disagree as to whether the arbitral tribunal has jurisdiction over the case (in its entirety or with regard to specific parts). Lack of jurisdiction may stem from a number of reasons: for example, the arbitration clause may be invalid (see II. 3.); the subject matter of the dispute may not be arbitrable at all; or the dispute may not fall under the specific arbitration clause. In such and other cases, the parties have the right to raise objections if they find themselves in front of an arbitral tribunal which, in their opinion, has no jurisdiction over the dispute.

As shown above, some legal systems allow parties to obtain a court ruling on jurisdiction before the arbitration commences. Many other legal systems allow parties to take their objections to the state courts once the arbitration has commenced. Under Article 16 (3) of the Model Law, the procedure is as follows: if a party raises objections as to jurisdiction, the tribunal may rule on these either in a separate, preliminary award or in the final award. If the tribunal confirms its jurisdiction in a preliminary award, the party may take the issue of jurisdiction to the state courts.

The Model Law stipulates that a party has to raise its objections no later than the submission of the statement of defense, or at least without undue delay; otherwise the party is precluded with these objections. In many legal systems, failure to meet these time limits means that the party cannot use the lack of jurisdiction as a basis to later have the final award set aside, or to block enforcement. Parties should therefore consider possible objections as to jurisdiction at their earliest convenience.

The arbitral tribunal is at liberty to proceed with the arbitration while the state courts are pondering the matter – or, indeed, to defer the decision until the final award. However, tribunals are well advised to take objections as to jurisdiction seriously: if there is any merit to the objections, a tribunal risks having its final award set aside (see VIII.). In practice, it will usually be preferable to deal with such objections in a timely manner, i. e. in a preliminary award.

The second important example in which a party to an arbitration may seek the assistance of the state courts is the challenge against arbitrators (see III. 6). Under most arbitration rules, and just as with objections as to jurisdiction, such challenges involve two stages. In the first stage, the challenge is resolved according to the procedure that the parties have agreed upon before. Such an agreement is usually reached implicitly, i. e. by the parties' agreement to institutional arbitration, because arbitration institutions – through their rules – provide procedures and mechanisms for resolving challenges.

If a challenge is unsuccessful at this first stage, the challenging party may then take the matter to the state courts. The Model Law leaves it to the enacting states to specify which courts should be responsible for challenges. However, the Model Law suggests that responsibility for challenges, for jurisdictional objections, and for setting aside proceedings should all rest with the same court. In many jurisdictions, this will be a court at the seat of arbitration.

Just as with jurisdictional objections, the arbitral tribunal may proceed with the arbitration while the state courts are dealing with the challenge. However, the tribunal thereby takes the risk that all efforts made in the meantime are rendered futile if the challenge ultimately succeeds in the state courts. This is because an award issued with the participation of the rejected arbitrator will be unenforceable in many jurisdictions. The German Federal Court of Justice, for example, has held that such an award can be set aside even if it was issued unanimously – on the grounds that it is impossible to rule out that the tribunal would have come to a different conclusion with a different arbitrator (decision of the German Federal Court of Justice, 11 December 2014, I ZB 23/14). Therefore, just as with jurisdictional objections, tribunals may find it preferable to wait for the court to resolve the challenge first, at least if a resolution can be expected within a reasonable time.

8. STATE COURTS MAY BE RELIED ON TO ASSIST WITH THE PRODUCTION OF EVIDENCE FOR ARBITRAL PROCEEDINGS

A party to an international arbitration proceeding may find itself in a situation where it has to rely on evidence that is not in its possession or otherwise beyond its control. Examples would include documents that are in the possession of the opposing party or a third party, or witnesses who are beyond the party's reach. The party may convince the arbitral tribunal to issue an order to the effect that the evidence in question be provided (for documents, in particular, see V. 2 and V. 3). But what happens if the addressee of said order does not comply with it?

Often, this problem is solved by putting the burden of proof on the uncooperative party. In other cases, this problem may be resolved by the tribunal drawing adverse inferences from a party's refusal, e. g. the refusal to comply with a document production order. In a few cases, however, it will be necessary to force a party to the arbitration or a third party to submit the evidence.

As private dispute resolution bodies, arbitral tribunals do not have the power to force parties to submit evidence. Similarly, arbitral tribunals cannot force third parties to provide witness evidence. In both cases, the respective power rests solely with the state courts. Therefore – just as with the enforcement of interim measures –, arbitral tribunals have to turn to the state courts for assistance if a party does not voluntarily comply with the tribunal's orders. Of course, just as with interim measures, parties are well advised to comply even if they cannot be forced to do so.

The Model Law recognizes this need and provides that

> "[t]he arbitral tribunal or a party with the approval of the arbitral tribunal may request from a competent court of this State assistance in taking evidence"

(Article 27 of the Model Law). Similarly, many jurisdictions explicitly enable arbitral tribunals to request assistance, either through a provision similar to Article 27 of the Model Law, or through independently drafted provisions. In the latter case, some jurisdictions restrict the court assistance to specific measures, rather than employing the catch-all language of the Model Law.

Article 27 of the Model Law further states that

> "[t]he court may execute the request within its competence and according to its rules on taking evidence".

Courts – insofar as Article 27 of the Model Law has been implemented – are thereby referred to their domestic procedural law. As a result, the extent of court assistance may fall short of what the arbitral tribunal has ordered, as the domestic procedural law may be too restrictive to execute everything that the tribunal has ordered. For example, the domestic procedural law may not allow courts to order third parties to disclose documents in their possession. Another result is that the sanctions for disobeying the court's orders will vary, depending on the jurisdiction.

Very often, the prospective addressee of a court order for evidence will not reside at the seat of arbitration, but in some other jurisdiction. This is an almost inherent issue in international arbitration, where the parties frequently and deliberately pick a "neutral" forum where neither of them is seated. (This line of thought has contributed significantly to the popularity of e. g. Zurich, Stockholm and London as seats of arbitration.) In such cases, the question arises as to whether the addressee's jurisdiction allows for court assistance with foreign arbitral proceedings as well. Perhaps surprisingly, this is the case in only a few jurisdictions, most importantly Germany and (arguably) the US. Within these jurisdictions, arbitral tribunals – regardless of their seat – can request court assistance for the taking of evidence. Otherwise, arbitral tribunals must take the matter to the courts at the seat of arbitration, which in turn must request judicial assistance from the courts in the addressee's jurisdiction.

9. STATE COURTS MAY DETERMINE NON-ARBITRABLE PRELIMINARY CLAIMS

Legal disputes often involve not only one claim, but a whole portfolio of claims. Sometimes, the parties find themselves in a situation where some of these claims are arbitrable while others are not. At other times, the non-arbitrable issues need to be resolved first before the arbitrable claims can be resolved – for example when the status or legal capacity of natural persons is in question.

In most jurisdictions, a party that concludes that a part of its dispute is not arbitrable has two options, neither of which is particularly attractive. The first option is to untangle the non-arbitrable part from the arbitrable part through legal analysis and file two lawsuits, one with the state courts and one for arbitration. This option carries the risk that the court and the arbitral tribunal come to different conclusions as to the arbitrability. Furthermore, the opposing party will have the opportunity to pounce on any potential mistakes or legal uncertainties.

The second option is to take the entire dispute to arbitration and ask the arbitrators to decide what parts of the dispute they consider to be covered by their mandate. The arbitrators' competence-competence includes the question of whether the matter is arbitrable. To the extent that the matter is not arbitrable, the arbitrators must decline jurisdiction – under some domestic laws (e. g. Germany), they have to do so even if neither party raises the issue. When making their decision, the arbitrators will also have to consider that agreements to arbitrate non-arbitrable matters are usually held to be invalid. They will have to consider as well that arbitral awards that resolve non-arbitrable matters cannot be recognized or declared enforceable under the New York Convention (see VIII. 7).

However, if the arbitrators decide that they *do* have jurisdiction, then the Model Law (and the domestic laws that have implemented it) provides the opportunity for the parties to appeal and have a court issue a final decision on jurisdiction (Article 16 (3) of the Model Law). So, just as in the first option, the parties end up in the state courts. However, the party bringing the claim is not forced to start the proceedings by committing itself with regard to which part of the dispute is arbitrable and which is not.

Whether a claim is arbitrable or not depends on the applicable national law. While the applicable laws are often quite clear on this issue (as e. g. with the German prohibition of arbitrating employment disputes), the problem lies more in finding the applicable law. In determining the non-arbitrable part, state courts have to address choice-of-law issues that are judged quite differently by commentators and other national courts. Complicating matters further, non-arbitrability in a domestic context does not necessarily mean non-arbitrability in an international context. In fact, a jurisdiction declaring vast swathes of the legal landscape "non-arbitrable", thereby excluding them from international arbitration, would arguably go against the spirit of the New York Convention. Therefore, contracting states are restricted when limiting arbitrability, and can only do so in order to address specific public policy concerns (*cf.* II. 2). This restriction does not apply in the domestic context.

If the state court finds that a part of the dispute is non-arbitrable, then in some jurisdictions the dispute as a whole is deemed non-arbitrable, at least if both parts are so intertwined that they cannot reasonably be separated. In other jurisdictions, the arbitration may continue as a matter of law while the non-arbitrable claims are decided by the state courts. If, however, the decision on the non-arbitrable matter prejudices the arbitrable claims, arbitral tribunals usually have the authority to stay the proceedings until the state courts have reached their decision – and they often choose to do so.

Finally, arbitrability may also be an issue in set-aside proceedings or proceedings regarding the recognition and enforcement of awards. In this context, the question of whether or not a claim was arbitrable is necessarily answered by a state court, and only by a state court (see VIII. 7).

10. THE TRIBUNAL MAY ISSUE INTERIM AWARDS, PARTIAL AWARDS AND A FINAL AWARD

Much has been written about the conditions under which a decision qualifies as an "award", and what type of award. Rather than being a merely academic matter, this debate has far-reaching practical implications. In particular, the New York Convention applies only to awards; hence, a decision that is not an award within the meaning of the New York Convention does not enjoy the protection of that Convention. One situation in which this may become relevant is when the tribunal orders interim relief (see VII. 2).

Legal scholars and case law agree that the distinction between awards and non-awards is a matter of content, not terminology. A decision labeled "Order" may well qualify as an award if its content meets the requirements, and therefore enjoy the privileges granted by the New York Convention. Similarly, a decision labeled "Interim Award" may, in actuality, be a final award, if its content meets the relevant requirements. As mentioned before, in one example, a US court held that a decision labeled "Interim Order for Security" constituted a final award.

So what are the content requirements? An award within the meaning of the New York Convention is the final and binding resolution of the subject matters submitted to the tribunal. With the issuance of the award, the matter becomes *res judicata*. The effects are twofold: Positive, the award is binding and the final word on the resolved subject matter. Negative, there may be no re-litigation on the same subject matter (*ne bis in idem*). If a tribunal's decision is meant to have these effects, then it is a (final) award, regardless of the label that the tribunal has put on it.

A partial award fits this description just as well. The word "partial" merely indicates that the award deals with only some of the issues at stake, not all of them. A partial award is a final decision on the subject matter resolved therein – indeed, some tribunals issue "Partial Final Awards": it is just not the last decision that the tribunal will make in that particular arbitration. While the terminology may be confusing, partial awards are nothing special. The designation as "partial" has no meaning for the purposes of the New York Convention, it is merely a red flag for the reader that there are other issues that have not yet been resolved by that particular decision.

Partial awards are a tool that allows tribunals to decide a complex case step by step, resolving issues sequentially rather than in a single decision. For example, tribunals often decide to resolve the issue of liability first before addressing the quantum of damages. Partial awards are expressly mentioned as an option in many institutional rules and many domestic laws, but even without such mentions, tribunals are generally considered to have the power to issue partial awards. The only exception is when the parties have agreed that no partial award should be issued. However, this rarely occurs in practice.

Instead, the relevant distinction is between final awards on the one hand and interim awards on the other hand. (Again, the terminology is of no relevance: whether a decision is called "Interim Award" or "Interlocutory Award" or simply "Order" does not matter.) This distinction is relevant because interim awards arguably do not enjoy the privileges granted by the New York Convention (see VII. 2). An award is "interim" if it grants provisional relief only, i. e. when it is intended to be subject to potential subsequent revision by the arbitral tribunal. Such an award is final and binding only insofar as it finally disposes of a specific request for relief, i. e. the request for an interim measure.

VIII.

AWARDS AND ENFORCEMENT IN DOMESTIC COURTS

1. FINALITY OF THE AWARD IS MORE DEFINITE THAN A DOMESTIC COURT JUDGEMENT

"By choosing arbitration, the parties choose, in principle, finality. An arbitral award is not intended to be a mere proposal as to how the dispute might be resolved, nor is it intended to be the first step on a ladder of appeals through national courts."
(Blackaby, Partasides et al., Redfern and Hunter on International Arbitration, 2015, p. 569).

One of the frequently quoted advantages of arbitration is that the arbitral award is final and binding upon the parties. In this sense, the arbitral award is expected to be "*the final say*" in the dispute – with no opportunity to appeal the award before a superior court.

In principle, this expectation is justified. Most institutional arbitration rules do not provide for an opportunity to appeal an award rendered by an arbitral tribunal. In fact, these rules often expressly state that an arbitral award is final and binding upon the parties (e.g. Article 38 of the DIS Rules). Some rules even provide that the parties are deemed to have waived their right to "*any form of recourse*" against an award (Article 35 (6) of the ICC Rules; Article 35.2 of the HKIAC Rules). However, some permanent arbitration courts (often established for specific commodities) provide for appeal stages, e.g. the Arbitration Rules of the Grain and Feed Trade Association (GAFTA) in London. Also, national arbitration laws may allow the parties to agree on an appeal stage (which parties rarely do). On the other hand, domestic court judgments can generally be appealed to a superior court under the applicable rules of civil procedure. The higher court will then review the lower court's judgment both for procedural and substantive mistakes – and either render a superseding decision itself or refer the case back to the lower court for a new decision. In this regard, an arbitral award is more definite than a domestic court judgment.

However, a losing party in an arbitration has at least two options to defend itself against an arbitral award. First, the losing party may opt for a challenge of the award in the national courts and according to the national laws at the seat of the arbitration. The purpose of a challenge of an award is to have the competent national court annul (also called "*set aside*" or "*vacate*") the award, i.e. declare that the award is invalid. As will be explained below (VIII. 2), the grounds for setting aside an award are very limited and narrowly defined. Usually, other available remedies – if any – must be used before challenging an award. These remedies may include an appeal or an application for correction or interpretation of the award under the applicable arbitration rules (e.g. Article 36 of the ICC Rules).

Also, there are time limits for challenging an award. Under German law, for example, a challenge must be made within three months of receipt of the award (Section 1059 (3) of the German Code of Civil Procedure). While it is possible to have an award set aside, it is important to note that this rarely happens in practice.

As a second option, the losing party may resist recognition and enforcement of the award in any jurisdiction in which the winning party seeks to enforce it. The recognition and enforcement of arbitral awards is widely governed by the New York Convention. As the Convention has more than 150 member states, including the most important jurisdictions of the world (e. g. all EU member states, the United States, China, and the Russian Federation), recognition and enforcement of a foreign arbitral award is generally easier than recognition and enforcement of a foreign state court decision. To resist recognition and enforcement of an arbitral award, the party against which enforcement is sought can rely on certain narrowly defined grounds under Article V of the New York Convention. These grounds often closely resemble the statutory grounds for challenging an award under national arbitration laws (see VIII. 2 – VIII. 7).

As opposed to courts hearing an appeal, most courts in setting aside or enforcement proceedings will – in principle – not review whether the arbitral tribunal rendered a "*correct*" decision on the merits of the case. In other words, there is generally no *révision au fond* of the arbitral award during setting aside or enforcement proceedings (see VIII. 8 for a discussion of "*manifest disregard of the law*" as grounds for challenge).

2. GROUNDS FOR CHALLENGING AN AWARD ARE USUALLY VERY LIMITED

As set out above (VIII. 1), national laws at the seat of arbitration govern the procedure for setting aside an arbitral award. Therefore, one must look at the national laws to determine the grounds on which such a challenge may be based. While each state is of course free to adopt its own arbitration laws, many states have adopted – or at least were inspired by – the Model Law.

Pursuant to the Model Law, an application to set aside an arbitral award may be based only on narrow grounds which are exhaustively set forth in the Model Law. Save for minor differences, these grounds are taken from Article V of the New York Convention. This means that a party can essentially rely on the same grounds for an application to set aside the award as for resisting recognition and enforcement of the award.

These grounds are:

- incapacity to conclude an arbitration agreement or invalid arbitration agreement under the applicable law (see VIII. 3);
- the party making the application was not given proper notice of the appointment of an arbitrator or of the arbitral proceedings, or was otherwise unable to present its case (see VIII. 4);
- the award deals with a dispute not contemplated by or not falling within the terms of the submission to arbitration, or contains decisions on matters going beyond the scope of the submission to arbitration (see VIII. 5);
- the composition of the arbitral tribunal or the arbitral procedure was not in accordance with the agreement of the parties or – failing such agreement – was not in accordance with the national laws of the country where the arbitration took place (see VIII. 5);
- the subject matter of the dispute is not arbitrable under the national laws of the country where the arbitration took place (see VIII. 7); or
- the award is in conflict with public policy (see VIII. 7).

In addition, recognition and enforcement of an award may be refused under the New York Convention if the award has not yet become binding or has been set aside or suspended by the competent court of the country in which the award was made (see VIII. 6).

As the above list shows, the grounds for setting aside and refusing to recognize and enforce an award are limited and narrowly defined. Most of the grounds are of jurisdictional nature (e.g. invalid arbitration agreement) or relate to a lack of due process (e.g. failure to give a party the right to be heard). Most notably, neither the Model Law nor the New York Convention allow the setting aside or the refusal of recognition and enforcement of an award based on a "*wrong*" decision on the merits, i.e. a mistake of fact or law by the arbitral tribunal. This means that by choosing arbitration, parties in many jurisdictions can "*contract out*" of substantive control by national courts at the seat of arbitration. Nevertheless, there are a few countries which allow the setting aside and the refusal of recognition and enforcement of an award if the competent court of that country finds that the arbitral award was wrong on the merits (see VIII. 8 for a discussion of "*manifest disregard of the law*" as grounds for challenge).

It is the prevailing opinion that the New York Convention does not impose any limits on the grounds for setting aside an arbitral award under national arbitration laws. Accordingly, some countries (e.g. the United States, England, Brazil) allow the setting aside of an award on grounds other than those set out above. However, there is a growing trend towards limiting the grounds to those exhaustively mentioned in the New York Convention. This is in line with what has been called the "*pro enforcement bias*" of the national courts, i.e. the vast majority of courts decide in favor of recognition and enforcement of arbitral awards.

3. INVALIDITY OF THE ARBITRATION AGREEMENT IS A REASON FOR CHALLENGING AN AWARD

Recognition and enforcement of an arbitral award may be refused if the underlying arbitration agreement is invalid, i. e. if

> "the parties to the agreement referred to in article II were, under the law applicable to them, under some incapacity, or the said agreement is not valid under the law to which the parties have subjected it or, failing any indication thereon, under the law of the country where the award was made"

(Article V (1) lit. a of the New York Convention). For the same reasons, an award may be set aside at the seat of arbitration under Article 34 (1) lit. a (i) of the Model Law.

In case an arbitration agreement is invalid, it is appropriate to deny recognition and enforcement of the award in accordance with the general principle of party autonomy in international arbitration. An arbitral tribunal has no authority to decide a dispute unless the parties have validly agreed to resolve the dispute by arbitration.

An arbitration agreement may be invalid because one of the parties was not allowed under the applicable law to enter into the agreement (i. e. had no capacity). In general, any natural or legal person (acting through its executive body) who has the capacity to enter into a contract also has the capacity to enter into an arbitration agreement. Special problems may arise if states or state agencies are involved, because some states are not allowed to refer disputes among themselves or between their agencies and a private party to arbitration. However, it will often be contrary to general principles of good faith and estoppel if a state invokes its own laws to argue that it had no capacity to conclude an arbitration agreement which it had previously voluntarily entered into.

The requirements of a valid arbitration agreement were discussed above (II.). An arbitration agreement is invalid if it does not comply with mandatory form requirements. In particular, Article II of the New York Convention requires that an arbitration agreement be "*in writing*". Most courts have held that the requirements of Article II of the New York Convention must be satisfied in order for an arbitration award to be recognized and enforced. With regard to the substantive validity of arbitration agreements, general contract law principles apply (e.g.

fraud, mistake or frustration). For example, a party may be able to resist recognition and enforcement of an award if the party can establish that it has successfully contested the arbitration agreement.

It is important to remember that the arbitration agreement is presumptively separable from the commercial contract in which it is contained (see II. 9). This means that the invalidity of the commercial contract does not automatically render the arbitration agreement invalid. However, defects in the commercial contract may also affect the arbitration agreement. For example, if the commercial contract has never been validly formed because one party's signature was forged, this will also lead to the invalidity of the arbitration agreement contained in the commercial contract.

Careful attention must be paid to the applicable law which determines the validity of the arbitration agreement. A distinction must be made between (i) the law governing the formal validity of the arbitration agreement, (ii) the law governing the substantive validity of the arbitration agreement, and (iii) the law governing the capacity of the parties to conclude the arbitration agreement. According to the New York Convention, if the parties have chosen (expressly or implicitly) the applicable law, that law must be applied. Otherwise, as a default rule, the law at the seat of arbitration applies. It is relatively uncommon for the parties to choose the law applicable to the arbitration agreement. More often, the parties simply include a general choice-of-law clause in their commercial contract. This choice-of-law is sometimes interpreted to apply to the (presumptively separable) arbitration agreement as well. The parties' capacity to conclude an arbitration agreement is governed by "*the law applicable to them*". In this respect, the New York Convention resorts to the "*personal law*" of each party. For natural persons, this will usually be the law of their domicile. For legal persons (such as corporations), the law at the place of incorporation will usually govern questions of capacity.

4. VIOLATION OF THE RIGHT TO BE HEARD IS A REASON FOR CHALLENGING AN AWARD

It is a fundamental principle in international arbitration that each party must be granted the right to be heard, i.e. to present its case properly. Accordingly, an award may be set aside or recognition and enforcement of an award may be refused if

> "the party against whom the award is invoked was not given proper notice of the appointment of the arbitration or of the arbitration proceedings or was otherwise unable to present his case"

(Article V (1) lit. b of the New York Convention and Article 34 (1) lit. a (ii) of the Model Law).

An alleged violation of the right to be heard is the most frequently invoked reason for resisting recognition and enforcement of an arbitral award. Indeed, the wording "*was otherwise unable to present its case*" is intentionally broad so as to include all potential reasons why a party was not able to present its case. However, in light of the "*pro enforcement bias*" of the New York Convention, this provision is construed narrowly: a mere irregularity of the arbitral proceedings will not suffice. Rather, the party against whom the award is invoked must prove that the arbitral proceedings suffered from a serious and significant procedural unfairness. As a consequence, national courts have only in rare cases refused to recognize and enforce an award on this basis.

There is some debate as to the applicable standard according to which a national court should decide whether a party was provided sufficient opportunity to present its case. While some argue that the law of the recognition forum should apply, others interpret Article V (1) lit. b of the New York Convention itself as establishing a uniform international standard of procedural fairness. In any event, it is generally acknowledged that a national court cannot simply apply its domestic rules of civil procedure to determine whether a party to an arbitration was given proper opportunity to present its case.

It obviously depends on the specific circumstances of a case whether a procedural irregularity is serious enough to render an award unenforceable. For example, national courts have refused recognition and enforcement on the grounds that:

- a party was not provided notice – or provided only insufficient notice – of hearings or other essential steps in the arbitration (e.g. appointment of an expert);
- a party was not afforded its right to be heard in the oral hearing or was not able to attend the oral hearing for compelling reasons (e.g. danger to life);
- a party was prevented from commenting on crucial evidence or arguments of the opposing party; or
- the tribunal (or an arbitrator) lacked the required independence or impartiality.

In other cases, courts have refused recognition and enforcement when it was established that a party had not been afforded enough time to present its case. However, recognizing the arbitral tribunal's wide discretion, courts are usually hesitant to question the timetable set by the arbitral tribunal; it will therefore be difficult to demonstrate a serious procedural unfairness on this basis. The same is true with regard to the argument that the tribunal (or an arbitrator) prejudged a particular issue in the arbitration. This is very difficult to prove in practice. Furthermore, a party cannot derive from the right to present its case a right to receive the tribunal's preliminary view on how it plans to decide an issue.

Moreover, courts regularly do not follow the argument that a party was unable to present its case because it did not understand the language of the arbitration – at least if the party had agreed to that language or the tribunal had chosen the language according to the applicable arbitration rules. Nor will an award which is based on contradicting reasons be denied recognition and enforcement; as stated above (VIII. 1), national courts will generally not review whether an award is "*correct*" on the merits.

Many courts have held that the party against whom the award is invoked must show a causal link between the procedural irregularity and the outcome of the case. In other words: Recognition and enforcement will only be denied if it cannot be excluded that the procedural irregularity affected the outcome of the case. It will usually be sufficient to show that the award may have been impacted by the procedural irregularity.

It is important to note that any objections under Article V (1) lit. b of the New York Convention may be considered waived if the aggrieved party does not raise the irregularities during the arbitration immediately upon their occurrence.

5. EXCESS OF JURISDICTION OR NON-COMPLIANCE WITH THE PROCEDURE ARE REASONS FOR CHALLENGING AN AWARD

An arbitral award may also be set aside or denied recognition and enforcement if the arbitral tribunal has exceeded the jurisdiction vested in it by the parties. Pursuant to Article V (1) lit. c of the New York Convention, this is the case if

> "the award deals with a difference not contemplated by or falling within the terms of the submission to arbitration, or it contains decisions on matters beyond the scope of the submission to arbitration, provided that, if the decisions on matters submitted to arbitration can be separated from those not so submitted, that part of the award which contains decisions on matters submitted to arbitration may be recognized and enforced"

(see also Article 34 (2) lit. a (iii) of the Model Law).

Two scenarios can be distinguished in which an arbitral tribunal has exceeded its jurisdiction: Either (i) the tribunal has decided on claims or issues which are outside the scope of the arbitration agreement, or (ii) the tribunal has decided on claims or issues which exceeded or differed from those presented by the parties in the arbitration.

In the first scenario, the tribunal has decided on claims which are not subject to the arbitration agreement, for example claims which arise under a different contract or certain types of claims which the parties had excluded from the arbitration agreement (e. g. non-contractual claims). However, it is widely accepted across all jurisdictions that arbitration agreements are to be interpreted broadly. The underlying rationale is that prudent business people generally intend to have all disputes arising from a transaction resolved in the same proceedings. When in doubt, an arbitral tribunal will therefore decide in favor of including a certain claim in the scope of the arbitration agreement. In the context of recognition and enforcement, many national courts have held that substantial deference must be given to the arbitral tribunal's decision regarding the scope of the arbitration agreement.

In some cases, parties have raised an alleged substantive claim as an excess of jurisdiction by the tribunal. National courts do not follow this reasoning. For example, if the parties have excluded in their commercial contract the right to claim punitive damages, an award of such damages will not be considered an excess of jurisdiction of the arbitral tribunal; rather, the award is simply incorrect on the merits. Similarly, if an arbitral tribunal applies laws to which the parties did not agree in their choice-of-law agreement, this may be wrong on the merits, but it is not a reason to resist recognition and enforcement of the award. On the other hand, if the arbitral tribunal decides the case as *amiable compositeur* or *ex aequo et bono* (this means without strictly applying the law) without being authorized to do so, this may constitute an excess of jurisdiction. In practice, however, the tribunal will seldom decide in this manner without having been authorized to do so by the parties.

Pursuant to the clear wording of Article V (1) lit. c of the New York Convention, an arbitral award may also be partially recognized and enforced where the part which exceeds the tribunal's jurisdiction can be separated from the part which is within the tribunal's jurisdiction.

Any objection under Article V (1) lit. c of the New York Convention may be considered waived if the aggrieved party does not raise the objection in a timely manner during the arbitration.

Finally, an award may also be set aside or denied recognition and enforcement if the composition of the arbitral tribunal or the arbitral procedure was not in accordance with the agreement of the parties (subject to mandatory provisions of the Model Law), or – failing such agreement – was not in accordance with the national laws of the country in which the arbitration took place (Article V (1) lit. d of the New York Convention and Article 34 (2) lit. a (iv) of the Model Law).

6. VACATED AWARD IS A REASON FOR NON-ENFORCE-ABILITY

An arbitral award may also be denied recognition and enforcement if

> "the award has not yet become binding on the parties, or has been set aside or suspended by a competent authority of the country in which, or under the law of which, that award was made"

(Article V (1) lit. e of the New York Convention).

This objection – although seemingly straightforward – has caused significant debate and quite divergent court decisions.

With regard to the first alternative, the question arises as to when an award has become "*binding*" on the parties. The New York Convention does not answer this question. While some suggest looking at the arbitration agreement to determine when an award is binding, others resort to the national arbitration law at the seat of arbitration. This law may contain certain formalities for an award to be binding, e.g. that each party has received a signed copy of the award (*cf.* Section 1054 (4) of the German Code of Civil Procedure). Other courts have held that an award is binding if it is no longer open to an appeal on the merits – either before an appellate arbitral tribunal or before a court at the seat of arbitration (if applicable, see VIII. 1). At least two points seem to be settled: (i) the winning party need not "*confirm*" the arbitral award in the courts of the seat of arbitration for the award to be binding; and (ii) neither a pending nor a possible future action to set aside the award prevents the award from being binding.

With regard to the second alternative, it will usually be easy to ascertain whether an award was set aside by a court at the seat of arbitration. For the reasons explained above (VIII. 2), it is quite rare in practice that an award is in fact set aside. However, in those cases where an award has indeed been set aside at the seat of arbitration, courts have reached different conclusions as to whether such an award can still be recognized and enforced in a different jurisdiction. At the outset, the clear language of Article V (1) of the New York Convention indicates that recognition and enforcement of an award "*may be refused*" if the award has been set aside. This means that courts have discretion to recognize and enforce an arbitral award even if it has been set aside at the seat of arbitration.

Some European courts (especially French courts) have recognized and enforced arbitral awards which had previously been set aside at the seat of arbitration. Many of these decisions rely on Article VII of the New York Convention, which allows a party to seek enforcement of an award under the national law of the enforcement jurisdiction if this national law is more favorable to recognition and enforcement than the New York Convention. Thus, if the national law does not consider the setting aside of an award to be grounds for refusing recognition and enforcement of such award, the winning party will likely be able to enforce the award in that country although it has been set aside at the seat of arbitration.

On the other hand, the majority of courts seem to deny recognition and enforcement of awards which have been set aside elsewhere. These decisions are based on the argument that an award is null and void once it has been set aside and therefore should not be recognized. Some courts also employ principles of international comity to explain their deference to setting aside decisions rendered in other jurisdictions.

7. VIOLATION OF PUBLIC POLICY IS A REASON FOR CHALLENGING AN AWARD

Pursuant to Article V (2) of the New York Convention, recognition and enforcement of an award may also be refused if the

> "recognition or enforcement of the award would be contrary to the public policy"

of the country in which recognition and enforcement is sought or if the

> "subject matter of the difference is not capable of settlement by arbitration under the law of that country".

These reasons are mirrored in Article 34 (2) lit. b of the Model Law. The reasons for attacking an award which are set out above (VIII. 3. – VIII. 6) will only be considered by the court dealing with setting aside or enforcement proceedings if a party relies on them. In contrast, the court may consider non-arbitrability or a public policy violation even if this is not brought forward by a party.

The circumstances under which a dispute is non-arbitrable have already been explained (II. 2). Public policy is frequently invoked as a defense by the losing party. In the majority of cases, this defense fails. Unlike the reasons for refusing recognition and enforcement under Article V (1) of the New York Convention mentioned above, public policy concerns may be raised by the national courts *ex officio*. In practice, however, the losing party will likely raise the objection on its own initiative. In any case, the losing party bears the burden of proof that the award should not be recognized and enforced due to a violation of public policy.

It is generally accepted that the New York Convention provides for the application of an international, rather than a purely domestic, standard of public policy. The prevailing opinion is that the international standard of public policy should be narrower than the domestic standard in the country in which recognition and enforcement is sought. On the other hand, Article V (2) lit. b of the New York Convention is intended to be a measure of last resort for national courts to give effect to their local law and policy. Against this background, national courts rely, in practice, on their local public policy, often described as the most fundamental principles of a country's legal and economic system. In doing so, national courts are very reluctant to apply the public policy objection; thus, the objection is rarely successful.

While perceptions of public policy may, of course, vary in different jurisdictions, some situations usually justify recourse to the public policy objection. A distinction can be made between procedural and substantive public policy.

It is usually considered a violation of procedural public policy if the award was obtained in proceedings which were contrary to the most basic concepts of procedural fairness, e. g. in case of fraudulent behavior. Some courts have ruled that such grave unfairness also exists if the arbitral tribunal was not impartial or if one party had greater influence on the composition of the tribunal. Other courts, however, have ruled that these defects were not part of public policy. Other procedural defects have also been rejected as public policy defenses, e. g. a party's lack of legal representation, failure to provide adequate notice, and the alleged failure to consider submitted evidence. Some of these defects are arguably already covered by Article V (1) lit. b of the New York Convention (see VIII. 4).

A violation of substantive public policy is usually assumed if the fulfillment of the award would be contrary to mandatory laws that protect the basis of public order in the country in which recognition of enforcement is sought. Accordingly, it would be contrary to public policy if the award required a party to commit a criminal offence or violate anti-corruption or bribery laws. Some courts have ruled that non-compliance with mandatory economic laws (e. g. European competition laws) may also constitute a violation of public policy. Awards of punitive damages have been considered to be contrary to public policy in some jurisdictions as well. In other cases, even the violation of basic principles of contract law (*pacta sunt servanda*, principle of good faith) has been considered to be contrary to public policy.

In sum, a violation of public policy is only assumed by national courts in rare cases. In particular, a mere misapplication of the law or a faulty legal reasoning does not amount to a violation of public policy. This is consistent with the notion that the award is generally not subject to a review on the merits.

8. "MANIFEST DISREGARD OF THE LAW" IS USUALLY NO REASON FOR CHALLENGING AN AWARD

It was already pointed out above that the reasons for setting aside and refusing to recognize and enforce an award are limited and narrowly defined. In particular, most jurisdictions do not allow the setting aside of an award or the denial of recognition and enforcement based on a "*wrong*" decision on the merits, i. e. based on a mistake of fact or law by the arbitral tribunal (see VIII. 2).

Contrary to this approach, under US law, an award may be set aside if it was rendered in "*manifest disregard of the law*". While the US Federal Arbitration Act does not explicitly provide for judicial review of an award based on a mistake of law, the doctrine of "*manifest disregard of the law*" emerged from the 1953 US Supreme Court decision in *Wilko v. Swan*. As applied in practice, an award may be set aside under this doctrine if (i) a governing legal principle is well defined and clearly applicable to the case, and (ii) the arbitral tribunal is aware of the principle and deliberately chooses to ignore it. Thus, a mere erroneous application of the law does not suffice.

Views on the doctrine vary widely among US courts. A number of lower US courts have refused to apply it altogether. Moreover, the US Supreme Court questioned the validity of the doctrine in its 2008 decision *Hall Street v. Mattel*, which has led to even more confusion in the application of the doctrine: some US courts have considered the *Hall Street v. Mattel* decision as an abandonment of the doctrine, while other courts have ruled that the doctrine is still applicable. In any event, there are only very few cases in which the doctrine has ever been applied. What is more, the vast majority of decisions have denied the setting aside of an award based on a "*manifest disregard of the law*".

While the US doctrine of "*manifest disregard of the law*" is based on case law, in England, a review of an arbitral award for mistakes of law is expressly provided for in Section 69 of the UK Arbitration Act 1996. Pursuant to this provision, an award may be set aside in case of serious mistakes of law. However, such review of an award is very limited. In particular, an award may only be reviewed if the parties have not agreed otherwise. This means that the parties can "*contract out*" of the review of an award for mistakes of law by English courts. Moreover, case law suggests that the court will only review questions of English law; if the law of another jurisdiction is applicable, an award rendered on that basis is out of the scope of review pursuant to Section 69 of the UK Arbitration Act 1996. Further, the decision on the question of law must "*substantially affect the right of one or more of the parties*". Finally, either (i) the arbitral tribunal's decision on the question of law must be "*obviously wrong*", or (ii) the question of law is "*one of general public importance*", and the arbitral tribunal's decision is "*at least open to serious doubt*". In accordance with these strict requirements for review, English courts have been very cautious in setting aside awards on the basis of mistakes of law.

A few other jurisdictions allow for a more or less expansive review of the merits of an arbitral award. These jurisdictions can particularly be found in Latin America and the Arab world. Most jurisdictions, however, do not provide for a review of the merits of an award – in line with the Model Law.

9. ENFORCEMENT PROCEEDINGS REQUIRE CAREFUL PREPARATION

In practice, the value of a claim turns on the claim's enforceability. When a party has obtained a positive arbitral award, it will usually request payment from the losing party on a voluntary basis. In most cases, the losing party will recognize its payment obligation and pay the due amount based on the ruling in the arbitral award. However, there are cases where the losing party refuses to pay – either because it does not have the means to pay or because it contests its payment obligation under the award, e. g. for one of the reasons set out above (VIII. 3. – VIII. 7).

If the losing party refuses to pay, the winning party must prepare to fight for enforcement of the award. Enforcement proceedings are often troublesome, time-consuming and expensive. Therefore, when deciding if and how to enforce the award, the winning party will have to weigh the benefits and costs before initiating such proceedings. If the expected costs of enforcement would eat up the payment claim under the award, the winning party should of course think twice.

In making the decision to enforce the award, the winning party will have to decide in which jurisdiction(s) it wants to seek enforcement. While enforcement proceedings can in theory be initiated anywhere in the world, one of the decisive factors should of course be whether the losing party holds any assets in a particular jurisdiction. In order to answer this question, it may be advisable for the winning party to engage a specialized asset tracing company which can identify any valuable assets the losing party may have. If, during the arbitral proceedings, a party suspects that the counterparty might try to hide or move assets, the party may request interim relief to prevent this.

In the international context, the losing party will often have assets in more than one jurisdiction. In this case, the winning party may choose to enforce the award in more than one jurisdiction, preferably in the jurisdictions with the lowest enforcement requirements and the fastest enforcement proceedings. The requirements and proceedings for enforcement are determined by national enforcement laws. It is therefore necessary to look into these national laws to determine the exact process of enforcement in a particular jurisdiction. Most notably, some national laws contain time limits applicable to actions for the enforcement of an award; such time limits may arise under the law of the arbitral seat and the law of the place of enforcement. The enforcement of an award therefore usually requires the assistance of local counsel in the jurisdiction(s) in which enforcement is sought.

The New York Convention contains certain formal requirements for the enforcement of an award. According to Article IV of the New York Convention, the winning party must provide a duly authenticated original of the award (or a duly certified copy thereof) and the original arbitration agreement (or a certified copy thereof). In case the award and/or arbitration agreement were not written in an official language of the country in which enforcement is sought, the winning party is further required to provide a translation into that language, certified by an official or sworn translator or by a diplomatic or consular agent. The practical steps for the enforcement of an award are set forth in more detail below (VIII. 10).

10. THE PROCEDURES FOR CHALLENGING AND ENFORCING AN AWARD DEPEND ON DOMESTIC LAW

PROCEDURE FOR CHALLENGING AN AWARD

It is not surprising that setting aside proceedings usually start with a corresponding application (cp. Article 34 (1) of the Model Law). According to the Model Law, such an application must be filed within three months after receipt of the award (Article 34 (3) of the Model Law). However, some national arbitration laws provide for shorter or longer deadlines. Many states provide that an application for setting aside can only be filed by a party who is aggrieved by the award, i. e. who has not fully prevailed in the proceedings. A third party can also be aggrieved in the exceptional case that the award's *res judicata* effect extends to the third party.

However, the Model Law does not address the details of the procedure for an action to set aside. Rather, these details were intentionally left to the states enacting the Model Law. In addition, it is up to the states to specify the court(s) or other authority competent to perform the setting aside procedure.

Article 34 (4) of the Model Law provides that, upon application of a party, the setting aside proceedings may be suspended in order to give the arbitral tribunal the opportunity to resume the proceedings or to take such other action as in the tribunal's opinion will eliminate the reasons for setting aside.

During the setting aside proceedings, it is open whether the award will finally be upheld. During this period of uncertainty, a need for interim protective measures may arise. If the award is quasi self-executing, e. g. excludes the losing party from an organization, that party may need protection. Or the winning party may have a legitimate interest in having the award provisionally enforced or at least in obtaining security that payment claims will be complied with if the award is upheld. Whether and how such interim protection is granted is determined by the state in which the award is challenged. German law, for example, provides for the possibility of preliminary enforcement which, however, may not extend beyond measures serving to provide security (Section 1063(3) of the German Code of Civil Procedure).

PRACTICAL STEPS TO ENFORCE A FOREIGN AWARD

As seen in the previous subchapters, the New York Convention sets forth the material grounds based on which recognition and enforcement of a foreign arbitral award may be denied. However, the Convention does not address the details of the enforcement procedure. Rather, the Convention merely contains rules on the burden of proof (Article V of the New York Convention) and lists certain documents which have to be submitted with an application for enforcement of an award (Article IV of the New York Convention, see VIII. 9 for details).

In addition, the party seeking enforcement must comply with the rules of the state in which enforcement is sought. According to these rules, the party may have to obtain a so-called apostille (= certification of the relevant documents by the consular authorities of the state in which enforcement is sought, located in the country in which the arbitration was seated). In addition, some states require notarization (= a testament by a notary public that the documents are in order). The applicant may also have to pay a substantial court fee or tax upfront. However, member states of the New York Convention must not discriminate against foreign awards and are therefore obligated to recognize and enforce such awards on terms that are not substantially more onerous than those imposed on domestic arbitral awards (Article III of the New York Convention).

Some states stipulate time limits (which, in some instances, are as short as three months) for the enforcement proceedings to be initiated. Neither the Model Law nor the New York Convention contain such time limits. Article VI of the New York Convention provides that the court in the enforcement state may adjourn the decision on the enforcement if an application for setting aside the award has been made at the seat of arbitration. In some states, it is possible to provisionally enforce an award despite setting aside proceedings pending at the seat of arbitration.

IX.

COSTS AND DAMAGES IN INTERNATIONAL ARBITRATION

1. ARBITRATION IS EXPENSIVE

Some in-house counsel believe arbitral proceedings are cheaper than state court proceedings. Others think that one of the main challenges to international arbitration is its inefficiency.

Both can be true. Arbitration can be cheaper than state court litigation, depending on the matter being heard in arbitration and depending on the alternative state court proceedings. State court proceedings in England, for example, are significantly more expensive than state court proceedings in Germany. State court proceedings in the United States can be extremely expensive when pre-trial discovery is permitted. In addition, state court litigation can be significantly slower because the parties can usually appeal the first decision. Arbitration, on the other hand, is one-stop adjudication.

However, arbitral proceedings can also have the potential to be significantly more expensive than state court proceedings. There are three main reasons why arbitral proceedings become overly expensive:

First, it is nowadays common practice in international arbitration that parties can ask for document production. This means: Both parties can demand that the other party produce documents or a category of documents regarding a certain subject matter, which are not in the possession of the requesting party (*cf.* V. 2). An example of a document production request is: "*all meeting minutes of Respondent's Board of Directors in financial year 2015*". Such document production requests are unknown in most civil law jurisdictions, but common in US state court proceedings. If document production requests are not narrowly tailored, they can result in the production of thousands of documents and waste a lot of money.

Second, arbitration hearings can take considerably longer than oral hearings in state court proceedings (at least proceedings in civil law countries) because more witnesses are examined and because the examination is not performed by the tribunal, but by the lawyers (*cf.* V. 5).

Third, arbitral proceedings can be more expensive than state court proceedings because there can be many rounds of written submissions. Arbitral tribunals are often reluctant to disregard unsolicited written submissions by the parties to avoid a later challenge of the award on the grounds that the tribunal has restricted one party's right to be heard.

The ICC, the leading arbitration institution, has published statistics on the average costs (*cf.* https://iccwbo.org/publication/decisions-on-costs-in-international-arbitration-icc-arbitration-and-adr-commission-report/). According to this,

- 83 % of the costs of the arbitration are party costs, i.e. lawyers' fees and expenses as well as expenses relating to witness and expert evidence
- 15 % of the costs of the arbitration are arbitrators' fees. Arbitrators are usually remunerated on the basis of a table of fees depending on the amount in dispute
- 2 % of the costs of the arbitration are the ICC's administrative fees.

Let's take the example of an arbitration with an amount in dispute of USD 20 million and three arbitrators. The average costs are:

- USD 2,100,000 in party costs
- USD 385,602 for the arbitral tribunal
- USD 67,515 for the ICC.

Statistics show that the biggest cost factors are party costs. The reasons for this have already been mentioned above. In order to reduce party costs, arbitral proceedings need to be managed efficiently, and the three causes of unreasonable costs should be tackled as follows: First, document production requests must be limited. Even if the tribunal decides to allow document production, document production requests should be narrowly tailored. Second, efficiently planned evidentiary hearings help reduce costs. Direct examination of witnesses should be replaced by written witness statements. Only witnesses relevant to the dispute should be cross-examined. Third, the parties should agree on a clear timetable for the arbitration and limit the rounds of written submissions. Unsolicited submissions should be admitted only in exceptional circumstances.

2. THE MEANS TO FORCE THE OTHER PARTY TO PAY THE ADVANCE ON COSTS ARE LIMITED

The parties must pay for the services of the arbitration institution and the arbitral tribunal. The amount to be paid is usually based on a fee schedule provided by the arbitration institution.

Under most arbitration rules, the parties are obligated to pay the advance on costs in equal shares at the outset of the arbitration. Article 37 (2) of the ICC Rules states:

> "As soon as practicable, the Court shall fix the advance on costs in an amount likely to cover the fees and expenses of the arbitrators and the ICC administrative expenses for the claims which have been referred to it by the parties … The advance on costs fixed by the Court pursuant to this Article 37 (2) shall be **payable in equal shares by the claimant and the respondent**".

By agreeing on the ICC Rules in their arbitration agreement, the parties also agree to comply with the obligation to pay the advance on costs in equal shares.

If one party defaults on the payment of the advance on costs, the other party is invited by the arbitration institution or the arbitral tribunal to pay the full advance on costs. It is usually the respondent that tails or returns to pay its share of the advance on costs. It is then up to the claimant to pay the respondent's share. If the claimant does not follow the tribunal's or the institution's invitation to pay the advance on costs in full, the tribunal may, under most arbitration rules, either stay the proceedings or terminate them completely. The ICC Rules provide that in this case, the claim is considered to be withdrawn. Article 37 (6) of the ICC Rules states:

> "When a request for an advance on costs has not been complied with, and after consultation with the arbitral tribunal, the Secretary General may direct the arbitral tribunal to suspend its work and set a time limit, which must be not less than 15 days, on the expiry of which the relevant claims shall be considered as withdrawn".

Thus, the claimant has no choice but to pay the entire advance on costs.

This raises the question of whether the claimant can demand immediate reimbursement from the respondent for the respondent's share of the advance on costs. Some arbitration rules specifically deal with this issue, e.g. the LCIA and the SCC Rules. Under Article 24.6 of the LCIA Rules, the LCIA Court may direct the compliant party to effect a substitute payment to allow the arbitration to proceed if the defaulting party fails or refuses to pay the advance on costs. If the compliant party effects a substitute payment, such party may request the tribunal to order the depoultry party to reimburse the advance on costs. Pursuant to Article 24.7 of the LCIA Rules,

> "the party effecting the further Advance Payment for Costs may request the Arbitral Tribunal to make an order or award in order to recover that amount as a debt immediately due and payable to that party by the defaulting party, together with any interest".

The answer to the above questions is open if the arbitration rules, e.g. the ICC Rules, do not specifically deal with the remedies of the compliant party. The majority opinion for the ICC Rules is that both parties contractually undertake to pay an equal share of the advance on costs. If one of the parties does not comply with this undertaking, the compliant party can substitute the defaulting party's share and request damages against the defaulting party. The tribunal could decide on such a request in a partial award.

According to a minority opinion, the breach of a party's promise to pay an equal share of the advance on costs generally has no legal consequences. Only in exceptional circumstances, provided that the claimant can prove that the requirements of an interim measure are fulfilled, could the tribunal order the respondent to pay or reimburse half of the advance on costs. Such exceptional circumstances could exist, for example, if the claimant would become insolvent if it had to substitute the respondent's share of the advance on costs. In all other cases, the claimant would have to bear the entire fees of the institution and the tribunal until the final award is rendered.

3. COST ALLOCATION USUALLY FOLLOWS THE FINAL AWARD

An arbitral tribunal has wide discretion as to which party should bear the costs of the arbitration. The majority of arbitral tribunals adopt, as a starting point, the rebuttable presumption that the prevailing party can recover its reasonable costs, in other words the principle of "*costs follow the event*".

This is confirmed by an ICC task force that has reviewed some 500 arbitral awards and analyzed the manner in which arbitral tribunals exercise their discretion (https://iccwbo.org/publication/decisions-on-costs-in-international-arbitration-icc-arbitration-and-adr-commission-report/). The analyzed awards were issued not only under the ICC Rules, but also under the rules of other arbitration institutions, such as CIETAC, HKIAC, DIS, ICDR, LCIA, PCA, SCC, and SIAC.

According to the ICC Report, tribunals allocated costs according to the "costs follow the event" principle despite the fact that the ICC Rules and at least half of the other major institutional arbitration rules do not contain a presumption in favor of recovery of costs by the prevailing party. Furthermore, the ICC Report points out that tribunals do adjust the event-driven allocation of costs. First and foremost, tribunals acknowledge an agreement by the parties on the allocation of costs. Tribunals also assess the reasonableness of the costs claimed by the prevailing party, the parties' procedural behavior, whether the parties have conducted the arbitration in an expeditious and cost-effective manner, as well as whether the parties have rejected an earlier settlement offer which would have led to a settlement avoiding the entire arbitration.

Irrespective of these findings, it is generally difficult to predict whether an arbitral tribunal will allow the prevailing party to recover its reasonable costs. There seem to be differences between the arbitration institutions:

- According to a previous analysis of 100 ICC awards rendered between 2006 and 2008, ICC tribunals do not tend to apply the "costs follow the event" principle as a starting point, but deviate from this rule in most instances. Ultimately, the prevailing party was able to recover its legal costs in only 63 % of cases (*Webster*, Arbitration International 2009, p. 469).
- While the above-mentioned ICC Report does not contain up-to-date statistics on ICC arbitrations, it does contain statistics on ICDR arbitrations (= International Center for Dispute Resolution in New York). In ICDR arbitrations, the prevailing party was able to recover its legal costs fees in only 26 % of cases.

- An analysis of 16 ICSID awards from 2014 and 2015, i.e. awards in disputes between a private investor and a foreign state, showed that only two tribunals accepted a pure "costs follow the event" approach. The tribunals were particularly reluctant to order the investor to pay the legal costs of the respondent state.
- In DIS arbitrations, on the other hand, it is generally accepted that the losing party has to reimburse the prevailing party's legal fees.

4. ALL COSTS ARE (USUALLY) RECOVERABLE

Just as important as the question "Who has to pay?" is the question "What fees and expenses can be recovered?". In general, all costs incurred in connection with an arbitration may be recoverable. The most important cost items are the parties' lawyers' fees.

- Usually, arbitral tribunals consider the actually paid hourly fees to be recoverable. In some jurisdictions, e. g. Germany, a prevailing party in state court proceedings cannot demand reimbursement of actual lawyers' fees incurred, but is limited to the fees calculated on the basis of a statutory fee schedule. The statutory fee schedule provides for a fixed fee based on the amount in dispute. In arbitral proceedings, no such limitation exists. Tribunals know that arbitration lawyers usually work on the basis of hourly fee arrangements. Hourly fees are therefore recoverable.
- Lawyers' fees are recoverable only if they are reasonable. In practice, arbitral tribunals compare the legal fees incurred by the claimant and the respondent. Unless they are totally disproportionate, they are recoverable in full. An arbitral tribunal will also take into consideration whether one of the parties had the burden of proof and therefore naturally incurred higher lawyers' fees.
- The parties should clarify with the tribunal how to substantiate their lawyers' fees in the cost submission. Usually, the parties present the cover sheets of all fee statements, the total number of hours worked, the total invoiced amount, and a confirmation from the law firm that the fees have been paid.
- In principle, the lawyers' expenses are also reimbursable, in particular travel expenses incurred for client or witness meetings or for oral hearings.

Moreover, it is common that witnesses who are not employees of a party, such as expert witnesses, are reimbursed for their time spent. No witness can be expected to meet with lawyers or to attend a hearing in his/her free time. As long as the reimbursement is reasonable, there are no ethical barriers to compensating witnesses. The costs as well as the expenses of the (expert) witnesses are also recoverable.

Finally, the costs of the arbitral tribunal and the arbitration institution are clearly recoverable, as are the logistical costs of the arbitral proceedings. Typical logistical costs are the costs for the hearing room, interpreters, and the court reporter.

Any other costs and expenses incurred by a party in connection with the arbitration are not recoverable. An exception might apply to the costs of in-house counsel. It is debatable whether these are recoverable (*cf.* IX. 5).

5. IN-HOUSE COUNSEL COSTS MAY BE RECOVERABLE

Arbitral proceedings require not only the attention and time of external lawyers, but also of in-house lawyers. A party's in-house counsel spends considerable time and effort on the arbitration, e.g. instructing its (external) legal representatives, assisting them with regard to factual issues, attending hearings, and keeping the company's management informed. Nevertheless, some tribunals seem reluctant to accept in-house counsel costs as part of the costs of the arbitration.

The arguments usually brought forward against recoverability are that costs for in-house counsel are part of the normal costs for running a business and that they would have been incurred anyway, since the company has its own internal, permanently established legal department. Very often, the time spent by in-house counsel is also not adequately recorded, and the applicable hourly rates are not known.

On the other hand, there are also valid arguments militating in favor of the recoverability of in-house counsel fees.

First, companies need to establish their own legal department only because of potential arbitration and litigation. In-house counsel are a crucial link between external counsel and the company that is a party to arbitration, because they can most efficiently provide external legal representatives with the input required from the client. Without the occurrence of litigation or arbitration, a company would not need to hire and pay in-house counsel.

Second, the time spent by company staff on the arbitration cannot be used for usual business activities and therefore qualifies as a cost.

Third, deeming in-house counsel costs unrecoverable could unjustifiably disadvantage a party that relies more on its internal legal department than on external legal representatives. In-house counsel will usually have lower hourly rates than external legal counsel, meaning that a party which is putting a large part of the workload on its own legal staff might actually reduce the costs of the arbitration. If in-house counsel fees were not recoverable, this could create an incentive to use expensive external legal counsel to a greater extent.

How should arbitrators and parties deal with the question of recoverability of in-house counsel fees in order to avoid surprises and misunderstandings at the cost stage of the arbitration?

1. Tribunals should discuss all potentially recoverable cost items (including in-house counsel fees) with the parties at the beginning of the proceedings.

In this way, tribunals can avoid two problems: first, that the parties omit to adequately record the hours spent by their in-house counsel; second, that disputes arise at the end of the proceedings over the general recoverability of in-house counsel fees.

2. If the tribunal has not made recoverable cost items part of the terms of reference, it should specify, at the latest at the close of the evidentiary phase, what proof a party needs to show in order to substantiate its in-house counsel costs.
3. Parties to an arbitration should keep a record of the in-house counsel's hours. This is particularly advisable because in-house counsel usually do not bill internally for their work and therefore do not keep a record of the hours spent specifically on an arbitration case. This may prove costly if the tribunal decides that the in-house counsel's costs have not been sufficiently substantiated.
4. If the tribunal, for its part, does not show any initiative to include recoverable cost items, such as in-house counsel fees, in the terms of reference, the party intending to recover such costs should push for them to be included.

6. SECURITY FOR COSTS IS DIFFICULT TO OBTAIN

What is the consequence if a party is sued without cause? As shown above (IX. 3), arbitral tribunals usually order the claimant to reimburse the costs of a prevailing respondent. What is the consequence if the claimant is ordered to reimburse the respondent's costs but refuses to do so? In this case, the respondent will have to enforce the arbitral award against the claimant. But what if it is clear from the outset that the enforcement against the claimant will be unsuccessful, e.g. because the claimant is a resident of a country that is infamous for its reluctance to enforce foreign awards, or if the claimant is impecunious? In this situation, the respondent will request security for its costs likely to be incurred in connection with the arbitration.

Security for costs can be obtained in state court proceedings in many common law and some civil law jurisdictions. If a respondent is entitled to security for costs, the court requires the claimant to deposit a sum of money with the court or provide a bank guarantee. If the respondent prevails in the litigation, the respondent can use the security to satisfy its claim for reimbursement of costs. If the claimant fails to provide security for costs, the claim is dismissed or treated as withdrawn. The idea behind ordering the claimant to provide security for costs is as follows: It would be unfair if the respondent was obligated to defend against a claim if the respondent knew from the outset that it will be unable to recoup its costs if it prevails. Security for costs may also be available in arbitral proceedings.

However, only a few arbitration rules specifically provide that a respondent may apply to the arbitral tribunal for security for costs, e.g. Article 25.2 of the LCIA Rules. While most arbitration rules are silent, such as the ICC Rules, there is still debate as to whether a tribunal can demand security for costs. The majority of tribunals have concluded that security for costs may be ordered by way of an interim measure. As with other interim measures, the respondent in the arbitration must show that there is a reasonable possibility that it will succeed in the arbitration and be entitled to reimbursement of its costs. Moreover, the respondent in the arbitration must show that harm not adequately reparable by an award for damages is likely to result if security for costs is not granted, and that such harm substantially outweighs the harm likely to be suffered by the claimant if security for costs is granted. This means: The respondent will basically have to show that it would not be able to enforce an award on costs (= irreparable harm).

Even if the respondent can meet this burden of proof, the respondent will in most cases not be entitled to a security for costs. Arbitral tribunals are concerned that they might limit the claimant's access to justice if the claimant is required to advance a large sum of money or procure a bank guarantee at the outset of the arbitration. In addition, arbitral tribunals take into account that the respondent has chosen to contract with the claimant, thereby accepting the claimant's impecuniosity or the claimant's residence in a country where the award cannot be enforced.

Arbitral tribunals therefore usually require proof of exceptional circumstances before ordering the claimant to pay security for costs. Such exceptional circumstances may exist, for example, if the claimant has dissipated its assets, the claimant has acquired a claim from the original contractual partner, or the claimant's financial situation has deteriorated dramatically since the date on which the arbitration agreement was concluded.

7. THIRD-PARTY FUNDING IS AVAILABLE IN INTERNATIONAL ARBITRATION

Only few in-house counsel view arbitration as an investment opportunity (*cf.* https://globalarbitrationnews.com/investment-arbitration-or-why-international-arbitrations-promise-a-solid-return-of-investment-20160413/). However, various third-party funders do! Third-party funders agree to finance the costs of an arbitration in return for a share of the outcome (between 10 and 30 %). Third-party funding can make economic sense both for claimants who could not otherwise "afford" to bring a claim and for claimants who have sufficient funds but want to mitigate their financial exposure.

Third-party funding was prohibited by law in numerous jurisdictions for many years. In common law, third-party funding qualified as "*champerty*", a punishable crime. Today, most countries allow third-party funding. Many countries also allow the funding of arbitration by lawyers through a so-called contingency fee. Under a contingency fee arrangement, lawyers provide their services for free or at a very low hourly rate. In return, they participate in the outcome of the proceedings. The reason why a contingency fee arrangement is not permitted in Germany, for example, is that it could create various conflicts of interest between the lawyer and the client. For example, a lawyer might advise a client not to accept a settlement proposal because the lawyer intends to "win big". Or a lawyer might file an unmeritorious claim or exaggerate the amount in dispute in the statement of claim instead of giving the client a true assessment of the chances of success. In other countries, such as the United States, contingency fee arrangements are very common. The advantage of a contingency fee is that it allows claimants – especially consumers – to litigate their claims without a financial risk.

In practice, third-party funding works as follows:

- Professional third-party funders are usually specialized insurance companies or funds.
- Before a third-party funder accepts to finance an arbitration, the third-party funder usually wants to review the claim's chances of success. Depending on the third-party funder, this review will be conducted either by the funder's own legal team or by an external lawyer. The claimant must provide all relevant documentation and assist the third-party funder in conducting a due diligence on the claim. Only if the claim promises a high chance of success will the third-party funder agree to fund the arbitration.

- If the parties to the dispute enter into settlement discussions, the settlement agreement needs to be approved by the third-party funder. If the third-party funder and the supported party disagree on whether to accept a settlement offer, a neutral umpire will decide.
- Depending on the agreement between the third-party funder and the supported party, the third-party funder may also be obligated to pay a share of the other party's legal costs if the other party prevails in the arbitration and is granted reimbursement of its legal costs.

Two specific concerns have been raised with regard to third-party funding in international arbitration:

First, the fact that a third-party funder covers a party's legal fees could have an impact on the independence of the arbitrators. It may happen that a party is funded by a third-party funder with whom one of the arbitrators has a conflict of interest. For instance, the arbitrator in an arbitration in which one of the parties is funded by a third-party funder could be the counsel to the claimant in another arbitration in which the claim is funded by the same funder. This impairs the independence and impartiality of the arbitrator and may have a direct impact on the valid constitution of the arbitral tribunal, which in turn may render the award challengeable.

Second, the fact that a claimant is supported by third-party funding could be evidence that the claimant is impecunious and therefore unable to pay an adverse cost award. As shown above, arbitral tribunals often allow the prevailing party to recover reasonable costs from the losing party (see IX. 3). However, the arbitral tribunal lacks jurisdiction to order the third-party funder to pay the adverse costs because the third-party funder is neither a signatory to the arbitration agreement nor a party to the arbitral proceedings. This may cause the self-funded party to request security for costs to avoid a situation where the impecunious award debtor cannot pay (see IX. 6).

In view of these concerns, there is controversy over whether a claimant must disclose the fact that it is backed by a third-party funder.

8. PUNITIVE DAMAGES ARE GENERALLY NOT AWARDED IN INTERNATIONAL ARBITRATION

Damages can be divided into two categories – compensatory damages and punitive damages. Compensatory damages compensate the claimant for a loss actually suffered. Punitive damages are awarded for an act or omission by the wrongdoer (the respondent) and to deter any future wrongdoing. However, the laws of most countries do not provide for punitive damages, especially for a breach of contract (which is the typical scenario in arbitration).

As the term implies, punitive damages penalize specific conduct. As such, punitive damages are an instrument of criminal law, not private law. Private law concerns the relationships between legal subjects and involves private interests. Criminal law, on the other hand, concerns the punishment and deterrence of criminal acts. With regard to criminal sanctions, most laws accord the defendants special constitutional protection. For example, criminal sanctions may be imposed only if they were expressly provided for in the law prior to the act in dispute (*nulla poena sine lege*). Moreover, the jurisdiction of the state criminal courts cannot be waived.

For these reasons, punitive damages are not only unavailable in most countries, but would even violate public policy. In 1992, the German Federal Court of Justice expressly decided not to enforce a judgment of a Californian court granting punitive damages because such a judgement violated German public policy. In 2007, the Italian Supreme Court rendered a similar judgment.

Arbitral awards granting punitive damages would violate the public policy of many countries that make the same distinction between private law and criminal law as Germany or Italy. Therefore, arbitral awards granting punitive damages would not be enforceable under the New York Convention in those countries. Moreover, if the seat of arbitration is in a country where punitive damages are unavailable, the arbitral award could be set aside by the state courts there. Under the Model Law, one reason for setting aside an award is that it violates the public policy at the seat of arbitration. Since punitive damages are unavailable and prohibited in most legal systems, arbitral tribunals rarely or never grant such damages in international arbitration. In fact, there is no single published ICC arbitral award that grants punitive damages.

Only in the United States and apparently also in Canada do arbitral tribunals have the power to order punitive damages. However, this power is rarely used.

First, the arbitral tribunal would have to be seated in the United States or Canada. Second, the applicable law would have to be the law of one of the US states or Canada. Third, the arbitral tribunal would have to exclude the possibility that the award would be enforced outside the United States or Canada. This leaves purely domestic disputes in which punitive damages might be available. But even in such purely domestic disputes, the parties to the contract containing the arbitration clause could agree to exclude the availability of punitive damages.

9. IN MANY JURISDICTIONS THE AWARD MAY NOT ESTABLISH PENALTIES IN CASE OF NON-PERFORMANCE

In most arbitration proceedings, the claimant asks for the payment of a sum of money – very often a claim for damages. In a number of cases, however, the claimant does not ask for monetary compensation, but for specific performance or injunctive relief. In such cases, the following question arises: can arbitrators provide for penalties or fines (also referred to as judicial penalties or "*astreinte*") in the event that the respondent does not comply with the order for specific performance or the injunction?

It is undisputed that arbitrators have the power to order the respondent to compensate the claimant for any damages resulting from non-compliance with the order for specific performance or the injunction. It is, however, less clear whether arbitrators may also impose fines or other penalties that not only compensate the claimant for any damages, but serve the purpose of incentivizing the respondent to comply with the specific performance or injunctive order in the first place. Opinions differ on the question of whether arbitrators have such authority:

In most jurisdictions, the law is silent on the arbitrators' power to order penalties. However, many scholars and courts, e.g. in France, agree that there is an inherent power. There are also some arbitral awards, e.g. the award in ICC Case No. 7895, in which the arbitrators make use of their power to order penalties. The reasoning behind this view is that arbitrators perform a similar function as state court judges. The French courts considered the power to impose penalties as an inherent and necessary extension of the jurisdictional function (*cf.* Paris Court of Appeal, 7 October 2004, Otor Participations et autres v. Carlyl). That is, if a tribunal has the power to order specific performance or injunctive relief, it is also that tribunal – and not a state court – that decides on the consequences if the tribunal's order is violated.

In many other jurisdictions, arbitrators seem to have no power to order penalties. There are two main reasons for this: First, a penalty that is meant as an incentive to the respondent and not as a compensation to the claimant could lead to an unjust enrichment of the claimant. This seems to be the main reason why arbitrators are not allowed to order penalties in common law jurisdictions. Second, a penalty or fine is a coercive measure. In some jurisdictions, such as Germany, coercive measures are reserved for state courts, and it is considered unconstitutional for arbitrators to encroach on the monopoly of the state. While there is no case law on this issue yet, it is likely that a German court would therefore not enforce a penalty ordered by an arbitral tribunal.

10. DEFAULTING ON THE OBLIGATION TO ARBITRATE CAN BE SANCTIONED

By signing an arbitration agreement, the parties undertake to submit their dispute to an arbitral tribunal and not to the state courts, in particular their home courts. If one party ignores this undertaking and initiates proceedings in the state courts, this constitutes a breach of the arbitration agreement. The question arises: What remedies does the other party have?

One effective remedy could be an anti-suit injunction (see VII. 5). Such an anti-suit injunction could be granted by a court or an arbitral tribunal. Alternatively, the party insisting on the arbitration agreement could request the arbitral tribunal to grant damages for a breach of the arbitration agreement.

Such a claim for damages is recognized in common law jurisdictions such as England or the United States. The English Court of Appeal has held that violation of an arbitration agreement is a "normal" breach of contract. The basic remedy available for a breach of contract under English law is a claim for damages. In the United States, the primary remedy for a breach of the arbitration agreement seems to be an anti-suit injunction. Therefore, case law on the claim for damages in this context is limited. However, it appears that arbitral tribunals in the United States also have the power to grant damages based on a breach of the arbitration agreement.

In Swiss law, it is debated whether an arbitration agreement is a procedural or a substantive contract. The Swiss Federal Supreme Court seems to take the view that an arbitration agreement is merely a procedural contract; a violation of this procedural contract could only result in procedural detriments. At the same time, the Swiss Federal Supreme Court held in 2013 that a tribunal seated in Switzerland and applying English substantive law could order damages for a violation of the arbitration agreement. Such an award does not violate Swiss public policy (judgment of the Swiss Federal Supreme Court, 30 September 2013, 4A_232/2013). Under German law, it is accepted that the arbitration agreement is both procedural and substantive in nature (decision of the German Federal Court of Justice, 28 November 1963, VII ZR 112/62). A violation of the arbitration agreement can, therefore, lead to a claim for damages.

The claim for damages must be submitted to the arbitral tribunal because the arbitration agreement is to be interpreted broadly and also covers disputes arising from a breach of the arbitration agreement itself.

In some cases, the damage resulting from the breach of the arbitration agreement may be obvious. If the state court seized in violation of the arbitration agreement dismisses the claim and refers the dispute to the arbitral tribunal, the "only" damage suffered by the respondent in the state court proceedings might be the costs of defending against the claim. Difficulties arise, however, in many other constellations, e. g. if the state court seized does not refer the case to the arbitral tribunal but renders its own judgment on the merits. This judgment could then contradict the arbitral tribunal's award on the merits. The arbitral tribunal in the case reviewed by the Swiss Federal Supreme Court (*cf.* above) granted the claimant in the arbitration proceedings/respondent in the state court proceedings a right to seek compensation from the recalcitrant party in the amount the respondent in the state court proceedings would incur to defend against the claim. The Swiss Federal Supreme Court saw no reason to deny recognition and enforcement of the award (judgment of the Swiss Federal Supreme Court, 30 September 2013, 4a_232/2013).

X.

AN INTRODUCTION TO INVESTMENT ARBITRATION

1. RESCUING SUNK INVESTMENTS – BITS CAN OPEN THE DOOR TO ARBITRATION AGAINST A STATE

Doing business in other parts of the world usually means entering a terrain of uncertainties. Is the political and legal system in the host state stable and reliable? Is corruption an issue? Will I be treated the same way as local entrepreneurs? If I feel that state authorities have violated my rights, can I expect fair legal proceedings? In many cases, the answers to these questions will not provide a high level of comfort.

Preferential treatment of local competitors, changes in legislation, or a simple decree issued by the government or local authorities may render an investment worthless. The prospects of legal proceedings before domestic courts in the host state may be limited for various reasons. However, the chances are high that the foreign investor can seek remedies before a neutral forum in arbitral proceedings by relying on a bilateral investment treaty ("BIT") or a multilateral investment treaty.

BITs are treaties entered into by two states with the objective of promoting foreign investment and protecting investment by nationals or companies of one state in the territory of the other state. Typically, a BIT requires both contracting states:

- to accord fair and equitable treatment ("FET") to investments of nationals or companies of the other state (see X. 9);
- to refrain from any discriminatory action and to accord those investments treatment not less favorable than the treatment the contracting states accord to investments of nationals or companies of the respective host state ("national treatment" or "NT") or nationals or companies of other states (most favored nation treatment or "MFN", see X. 4);
- not to expropriate the foreign investor without full, adequate, and prompt compensation (see X. 8).

Although these treaties are concluded between states, many of them establish the right of a national of one of the states to bring proceedings directly against the other state. This is commonly referred to as investor-state arbitration or investor-state dispute settlement ("ISDS"). Often, the foreign investor can even choose among a number of options, such as:

- ad-hoc arbitration under the UNCITRAL Arbitration Rules;
- ICC arbitration or arbitration under the rules of another arbitration institution such as the Stockholm Chamber of Commerce; or
- arbitration under the Convention on the Settlement of Investment Disputes between States and Nationals of Other States ("ICSID Convention"). The International Centre for Settlement of Investment Disputes ("ICSID") is part of the World Bank group and provides a set of rules for the settlement of disputes through conciliation or arbitration. A precondition for the jurisdiction of ICSID is a dispute between an ICSID member state and a national of another ICSID member state. For disputes that fall outside the scope of the ICSID Convention, ICSID provides its Additional Facility with a different set of rules.

There is a high probability that the investment at stake is protected by a BIT. Currently, there are more than 2,500 BITs in force.

In addition to BITs, there are multilateral treaties in place which provide a similar level of protection including ISDS. A prominent example is the Energy Charter Treaty ("ECT"). Fifty-two states, as well as the European Union and EURATOM have signed or acceded to the ECT. The Trans-Pacific Partnership Agreement ("TPP") is another example. There are quite a few more multilateral treaties providing for the protection of foreign investments.

Apart from BITs and multilateral treaties, ISDS can be based on dispute resolution clauses in agreements concluded directly between a state and a foreign investor on a particular project, e.g. a major infrastructure project. Moreover, some states have adopted so-called investment laws which provide a similar level of protection as well as dispute resolution mechanisms. The latter are a certain type of legislation which developing countries in particular have adopted to attract foreign investors.

Statistics show that the number of investor-state arbitrations has grown significantly since the mid-1990s. Nevertheless, the future of ISDS is uncertain. As a result of critical public debates some modern BITs are taking a more cautious approach with respect to the scope of investment protection and ISDS. UNCITRAL has entrusted a working group with the mandate to explore ways to reform ISDS. The EU is set to turn its back on the prevalent forms of ISDS, promoting instead the concept of a permanent multilateral investment court ("MIC"). Meanwhile, Canada and the EU have established the fundamentals of a so-called investment court system ("ICS") in their renegotiated Comprehensive Economic and Trade Agreement ("CETA").

As far as so-called intra-EU BITs are concerned, the *Achmea* decision of the European Court of Justice ("ECJ") has created a shockwave in the investment arbitration community. In that decision, the ECJ ruled that an arbitration clause in the Netherlands-Slovakia BIT was incompatible with the principle of autonomy of the EU legal system. As the EU Commission and the EU member states have agreed to embark on the termination of intra-EU BITs, it is fair to say that ISDS on the basis of BITs between EU member states will soon be history.

2. (ESTRANGED) SIBLINGS: THERE ARE DIFFERENCES AND SIMILARITIES BETWEEN INTERNATIONAL COMMERCIAL ARBITRATION AND INVESTMENT ARBITRATION

While commercial arbitration and investor-state arbitration have many things in common, there are also some fundamental differences between the two.

What do commercial arbitration and investor-state arbitration have in common? Both types of proceedings are usually governed by a set of institutional arbitration rules, for example the UNCITRAL Rules, the ICC Rules or the SCC Rules. Consequently, both commercial arbitration and investor-state arbitration follow a similar procedure for the constitution of the tribunal and the appointment of arbitrators. The conduct of the arbitral proceedings is also similar. There are notices of (or requests for) arbitration, there are submissions by the parties covering issues of jurisdiction, admissibility, and merits. Typically, there are case management conferences with the tribunal, there are hearings with opening statements and potentially closing statements, and evidentiary hearings with cross-examinations of witnesses and experts. If the claimant is successful and the respondent does not "volunteer" to comply with the award, the claimant will have to seek enforcement of the award in both commercial and investor-state arbitration (but see also X. 7).

What are the differences between the two types of arbitration? Put simply, commercial arbitration is mainly a matter of *private or commercial law*, based on the provisions of the underlying contract between the parties and the applicable substantive law as agreed in the contract. In contrast, treaty-based investor-state arbitration deals with matters of *public international law* in addition to the applicable law of the contracting states. It is about alleged breaches of provisions in treaties between states. The consent to arbitrate treaty claims is usually not based on an arbitration clause in an underlying commercial contract, but on an offer by the host state in a bilateral or multilateral investment treaty (see X. 3).

Investor-state arbitrations are often bifurcated, with the first part of the proceedings dealing with questions of jurisdiction and admissibility. This part of the proceedings is usually concluded with a decision on jurisdiction. The second phase of the proceedings focuses on the merits. The reason for such a bifurcation is that in most cases the respondent state raises a number of objections to the jurisdiction of the forum applied to and/or the admissibility of the claims. This is particularly true for ICSID proceedings.

While confidentiality is an important aspect of commercial arbitration, transparency plays an increasingly important role in investor-state arbitration. Through a publicly accessible case register, ICSID has always made information on the initiation of proceedings available. In addition, it has – with the consent of the parties – published awards or excerpts thereof and other documents issued throughout the proceedings. Pursuant to the ICSID Arbitration Rules, arbitral tribunals may accept *amicus curiae* briefs (e. g. by NGOs) and allow third parties to attend the hearings.

The UNCITRAL Rules on Transparency in Treaty-Based Investor-State Arbitration ("UNCITRAL Transparency Rules"), a product of the 2014 Mauritius Convention on Transparency, even go one step further. Subject to certain exceptions, they require submissions, awards and other documents to be published. They allow third party submissions and even public hearings, for example by video transmission.

As a result, a lot of information about investor-state arbitrations can be found on the internet, including awards and even submissions by the parties. This has some practical consequences, including the following:

- There is a considerable database of case law. Party submissions as well as awards contain numerous references to decisions rendered in other cases. In contrast, case law in commercial arbitration is scarce due to the mainly confidential nature of the proceedings.
- Thorough research of the published awards will affect the selection of arbitrators, as it allows to evaluate the approach of certain arbitrators to specific recurring legal issues.

Another peculiarity of investor-state arbitration is the nationality of the members of the tribunal. According to Article 39 of the ICSID Convention and Rule 1 (3) of the ICSID Arbitration Rules, the tribunal must not consist of a majority of arbitrators of the nationality of either the host state or the investor's state, unless all arbitrators have been appointed by agreement of the parties. In the case of a three-member tribunal, neither party may appoint a national of either state unless the other party agrees.

Last but not least, there are important differences in the challenge, recognition, and enforcement of an ICSID award compared to awards of tribunals constituted under other regimes (see X. 7).

3. THE CONSENT TO ARBITRATE TREATY CLAIMS – THE FIRST PART IS ALREADY THERE

Just as commercial arbitration, investor-state arbitration requires the consent of the parties to refer a dispute to arbitration.

Commercial arbitration is typically based on a contract with an arbitration clause. In this arbitration clause, the parties agree to refer disputes arising from the contract to arbitration. The arbitration clause expresses the parties' consent to arbitrate.

But how can consent to arbitrate be obtained between a state and a foreign investor? For investor-state arbitration, there are basically three ways by which such consent can be established, depending on whether the claims are based on a contract between the investor and the host state, on a treaty, or on investment legislation.

First, an agreement to arbitrate can be included in a contract between the investor and the state. Occasionally, investors enter into direct contracts with a state or a state subdivision. A typical example is the development, construction, operation, and/or maintenance of an infrastructure project in the host state. In such a contract, the investor may be able to agree with the host state to have all disputes between the parties in connection with the project decided by an arbitral tribunal. In addition, such an arbitration clause may refer to an existing investment treaty and clarify that the parties agree that the project constitutes an investment under the regime of that investment treaty. If the arbitration clause is intended to establish ICSID jurisdiction, some peculiarities need to be taken into account, as explained below.

Second, consent can be achieved on the basis of an investment treaty. In most investment treaties, the state parties express their consent to arbitration in the form of a "standing offer" to foreign investors. Attention must be paid to the exact wording of the relevant clause in the treaty. While most treaties provide for unconditional consent, others contain only promises of consent in the future. In some instances, consent may be limited to specific matters. In other cases, consent may be subject to preconditions, such as the exhaustion of local remedies, amicable settlement negotiations, and cooling-off periods.

In many cases, the foreign investor can accept this "standing offer" of the state by simply instituting proceedings in accordance with (one of) the arbitration rules referred to in the treaty. However, the investor may as well accept the state's offer prior to instituting proceedings, for instance, by way of written communication to the state. Again, the exact wording of the dispute resolution clause in the treaty is important. Some BITs require that the investor's consent be given before proceedings are instituted.

Third, consent may be derived from the investment legislation in the host state. If a state has adopted an investment law, the state's offer to arbitrate might be found there. While some investment laws provide for unconditional consent to arbitrate a wide range of disputes, others contain conditions or limitations similar to those mentioned above in connection with treaty-based arbitration. Often, it will be sufficient for the investor to accept the offer by instituting arbitral proceedings. In other cases, a separate acceptance prior to bringing the claim may be required. In fact, depending on the circumstances, an investor may be well advised to accept the state's offer at an early stage of the investment activities. This is because a state's offer to arbitrate under an investment law may suddenly cease to exist through a simple change in legislation.

In order to establish the jurisdiction of ICSID additional requirements must be met. First of all, the applicable treaty or investment law must provide for the possibility of ICSID arbitration. In addition, pursuant to Article 25 of the ICSID Convention, at the time of consent, the host state must be a party to the ICSID Convention, and the investor must be a national of a state party to the Convention. Given that 153 states have signed and ratified the Convention, the chances are quite high that these requirements are fulfilled. Issues are likely to arise when a state denounces the ICSID Convention, as Ecuador, Bolivia, and Venezuela have done. There are debates about the exact consequences of such a denunciation. In any event, there is a high risk that ICSID arbitration will not be available to an investor if the host state has denounced the ICSID Convention, unless the consent to arbitrate had been perfected through the acceptance by the investor prior to the denunciation.

4. MANY INVESTORS ENJOY PROTECTION UNDER BITS … AND THE OPPORTUNITY FOR TREATY SHOPPING

Who qualifies as a foreign investor? BITs and multilateral treaties define to which investors they extend their scope of protection. "Investors" usually comprise natural and juridical persons. While definitions vary, they typically include nationals of the other contracting state and corporations, partnerships or organizations incorporated or constituted in accordance with the laws of the other contracting state or having their seat in the territory of the other contracting state. Difficult issues may arise in case of a change of the nationality of an investor, complex cross-border shareholder structures, or a change in the structure of the investment in the course of a dispute.

The ICSID Convention extends the jurisdiction of ICSID to cases where the parties have agreed that "because of foreign control", a company should be treated as a national of another contracting state. For example: Company A is incorporated in the host state. Company B, which holds 80 % of the shares in company A, is seated in another state. Although company A is a domestic company, it could still be treated as "foreign". The question of when an investment in a contracting state is "controlled" by a company or individual of the other contracting state must be decided on a case-by-case basis. This depends very much on the exact wording of the relevant provisions in the underlying treaty.

A well advised investor planning business activities abroad will consider structuring the investment to benefit from the protection of an investment treaty. For example: If there is no investment treaty in place between the host state and the state where the investor's company is seated, the investor may structure the investment via a company seated in another state that has concluded such a treaty with the host state. Structuring an investment with the objective of optimizing investment protection through investment treaties is often referred to as "treaty shopping". Although the phenomenon of treaty shopping has raised some concerns, structuring an investment to benefit from treaty protection is usually not considered to be abusive. There are, however, exceptions to this rule in the case of fraudulent behavior of the investor. It must also be borne in mind that treaty protection does not apply retroactively. Thus, tribunals have rejected claims or declined jurisdiction in cases where an investment was restructured for reasons of BIT protection at a time when the host state had already committed a breach or a dispute had already emerged.

The term "treaty shopping" is also used in another context: most investment treaties contain so-called Most Favored Nation ("MFN") clauses. These are provisions by which states undertake to treat investments by investors of the other contracting state not less favorably than investments by investors from any other state. Such a provision allows an investor from state A to invoke provisions of a BIT concluded between the host state and state B if the latter is more beneficial than the BIT between state A and the host state. For example: If an investor from Canada makes an investment in the host state and finds that a BIT between the host state and Japan is more beneficial than the BIT between the host state and Canada, the investor might be entitled to rely on provisions in the former by virtue of the MFN clause in the latter.

There has been quite some debate about the question of whether the operation of MFN is restricted to substantive rights or whether it also extends to aspects of jurisdiction and admissibility of a claim. For example: Can an investor seeking to bring a claim under the BIT between his home state and the host state rely on the provisions of another BIT entered into by the host state, if the latter BIT makes it easier for the investor to bring such a claim? *Maffezini v. Spain* is one of the landmark cases in which the tribunal accepted to apply MFN to matters of jurisdiction and admissibility. While some tribunals followed the reasoning of the tribunal in *Maffezini*, others refused to apply MFN clauses for the purpose of extending the scope of the ICSID jurisdiction.

5. NUMEROUS KINDS OF INVESTMENTS ARE PROTECTED

What kinds of commercial activities or assets in the host state are protected? When bringing a claim in a treaty-based investor-state arbitration, an investor must establish that the respective activities or assets in the host state are within the scope of protection of the relevant BIT or multilateral treaty. In other words, the investor must demonstrate that those activities or assets constitute an investment protected by the treaty.

Many investment treaties include a very broad definition of "investment", followed by a non-exhaustive list of examples. The following typical example is taken from the Chile-Switzerland BIT:

> The term "investment" shall include every kind of asset and particularly:
>
> (a) movable and immovable property as well as any other rights in rem, such as servitudes, mortgages, liens, pledges;
>
> (b) shares, parts or any other kinds of participation in companies;
>
> (c) claims to money or to any performance having an economic value;
>
> (d) copyrights, industrial property rights (such as patents, utility models, industrial designs or models, trade or service marks, trade names, indications of origin), know-how and goodwill;
>
> (e) concessions under public law, including concessions to search for, extract or exploit natural resources as well as all other rights given by law, by contract or by decision of the authority in accordance with the law.

Such a broad definition of "investment" has given rise to concerns about an extension of treaty protection to all sorts of simple, one-time commercial transactions. Therefore, other investment treaties take a more restrictive approach in order to exclude short-term transactions such as one-time sales of goods or services, certain types of loans in connection with commercial transactions, and certain types of claims for money.

An investor wishing to institute ICSID arbitration must establish that the activities in question qualify as an investment under the ICSID Convention. Article 25 of the ICSID Convention provides jurisdiction only for disputes arising directly out of an investment. While the Convention does not define the term "investment", there is wide agreement that not each and every commercial transaction constitutes an investment under the ICSID Convention.

In an attempt to define the characteristics of an investment, many tribunals have adopted, either directly or with some modifications, the so-called *Salini* test, named after the tribunal's decision on jurisdiction in *Salini v. Morocco*. Pursuant to the *Salini* test, essential features of an investment are (a) a contribution in the form of assets, money, know-how, or the like, (b) a certain duration of the investment, (c) an element of risk, and (d) a contribution to the host state's economic development. The dispute in *Salini* was about allegedly outstanding remuneration for the construction of a motor highway in Morocco, which the involved state-controlled entity had refused to pay. The tribunal found that all of the above-stated requirements were fulfilled: It held that *Salini* had made contributions in the form of knowhow, equipment, personnel, etc. It further considered 36 months of construction works sufficient to meet the duration requirement. The tribunal stressed that the project involved elements of risk, such as potential increases in the scope of work which would not necessarily result in an entitlement to additional remuneration, and finally that the project constituted a significant contribution to the host state's development.

While some tribunals have modified the *Salini* test, it is still frequently used at least as a starting for the discussions on jurisdiction.

6. THE INVESTOR MAY CHOOSE THE FORUM, BUT MUST BE AWARE OF THE FORK IN THE ROAD

As explained above (see X. 1), many BITs and multilateral treaties invite the investor to choose among a number of options to pursue claims. Depending on the treaty, these options may include local courts, ICSID arbitration, ICC arbitration, UNCITRAL arbitration, SCC arbitration, or others. Some treaties limit the choices so that once the investor has selected one route, e.g. litigation before state courts, the investor is prevented from pursuing the same claims in another forum, e.g. arbitration. This is often referred to as a "*fork in the road*" clause, which might look like the following example:

1. A national or company that is a party to an investment dispute may submit the dispute for resolution under one of the following alternatives:

   (a) to the courts or administrative tribunals of the Party that is a party to the dispute; or

   (b) in accordance with any applicable, previously agreed dispute settlement procedures; or

   (c) in accordance with the terms of paragraph 2.

2. Provided that the national or company concerned has not submitted the dispute for resolution under paragraph 1 (a) or (b), the national or company concerned may submit the dispute to:

   (a) the International Centre for Settlement of Investment Disputes (ICSID) if both Contracting Parties are parties to the ICSID Convention,

   (b) a sole arbitrator or ad hoc arbitration tribunal established under the UNCITRAL Arbitration Rules,

   (c) an arbitral proceeding under the Rules Arbitration Institute of the Stockholm Chamber of Commerce, or

   (d) if agreed by both parties to the dispute, to any other arbitration institution or in accordance with any other arbitration rules.

If an investor has pursued claims before a local court of the host state and then pursues those claims in subsequent investor-state arbitration, the respondent state is likely to raise a jurisdictional objection on the basis of the fork in the road clause in the investment treaty.

For example: A technology company has entered into a contract with the government of the host state about the implementation and operation of a road toll system in the host state. In this contract (= the investment agreement), the parties have agreed to resolve disputes before a tribunal constituted in accordance with the rules of the national arbitration institution. After the implementation of the toll system, the host state terminates the investment agreement, thus depriving the investor of the opportunity to generate profit by operating the toll system. In the initial proceedings, the investor pursues the claims against the host state for breach of contract in national arbitration, as provided for in the investment agreement. Later, the investor institutes ICSID arbitration, invoking the fair and equitable treatment obligations under a BIT. In the latter proceedings, the host state raises judicial objections on the basis of a fork in the road clause in the BIT.

A tribunal faced with such a fork in the road objection will have to examine whether the *same* claim has been or is being pursued in different judicial fora. Sometimes tribunals apply a so-called triple identity test: same party, same object, and same cause of action.

Very often, tribunals have dismissed fork in the road objections raised by the respondent states. The rationale behind these rulings is that there is a distinction between the nature of a claim based on a contract (the investment agreement) and the nature of a claim based on a treaty (e. g., a BIT). Other arbitral tribunals have granted the respondent state's objection on the basis that the claims previously pursued before a local forum had the same "fundamental basis" as the claims pursued in the investor-state arbitration. (For the distinction between contract claims and treaty claims, see also Chapter X. 10.)

7. RECOGNITION AND ENFORCEMENT OF ICSID AWARDS IS RELATIVELY EASY

A state defeated in an investor-state arbitration is likely to comply with the award. Non-compliance would send deterrent signals to foreign investors with far-reaching impacts on the investment climate in that state.

However, there have been instances where states have refused to pay the investor the amounts due under the award. In such cases, the investor is left with no choice but to seek recognition and execution of the award. A claimant holding an ICSID award benefits from several advantages, as the award is not subject to any review by the local courts of ICSID member states.

Instead, the ICSID regime provides for a self-contained system with an internal procedure of judicial review, ranging from supplementation/rectification (of simple technical errors in an award) to annulment. The latter is restricted to five grounds listed in Article 52 (1) of the ICSID Convention. These five grounds are:

- The tribunal was not properly constituted.
- The tribunal manifestly exceeded its powers.
- There was corruption on the part of a member of the tribunal.
- There was a serious departure from a fundamental rule of procedure.
- The award fails to state the reasons on which it is based.

No other remedies are available. Article 54 (1) of the ICSID Convention establishes the general obligation of each member state to recognize and enforce ICSID awards:

> "Each Contracting State shall recognize an award rendered pursuant to this Convention as binding and enforce the pecuniary obligations imposed by that award within its territories as if it were a final judgement of a court in that State. (…)".

Thus, the recognition of an ICSID award is not left to domestic laws. It is also independent from the New York Convention. ICSID member states must recognize and enforce pecuniary obligations imposed by a final ICSID award "*as if it were a final judgement of a court in that State*". Domestic courts of a member state may not re-examine an ICSID award in terms of jurisdiction, procedure, or merits. Not even a public policy violation would constitute a valid reason to challenge the award. Enforcement as such is done in accordance with the rules of the state in which enforcement is sought. Enforcement proceedings may be initiated in several states at the same time.

Pursuant to Article 54 (2) of the ICSID Convention, ICSID member states have designated courts or other authorities as competent for the recognition and enforcement of ICSID awards. The list of competent courts and authorities can be found on the ICSID website.

While recognition of an ICSID award is usually straightforward, problems can arise in search for assets suitable for enforcement. The ICSID Convention does not contain a waiver of the state immunity from execution. Article 55 of the ICSID Convention provides that

> "[n]othing in Article 54 shall be construed as derogating from the law in force in any Contracting State relating to immunity of that State or of any foreign State from execution".

In other words, the award can only be enforced against assets which are not protected by state immunity under the law of the state in which enforcement is sought. Generally speaking, an investor trying to enforce an award against a state will only be able to seize commercial assets, as opposed to assets serving administrative or governmental purposes, such as embassy facilities. This is a challenge that an investor faces whether seeking to enforce an ICSID award or any other arbitral award.

8. NO EXPROPRIATION WITHOUT COMPENSATION!

Being expropriated is one of the greatest fears of any investor doing business abroad. Against this background, it does not come as a surprise that expropriation scenarios play an important role in investment protection. While BITs and multilateral investment treaties cannot prevent expropriation or nationalization, they provide the investor with the means to seek adequate and effective compensation when expropriation or nationalization has occurred. In other words, the treaties address the conditions and consequences of expropriations rather than their general prevention. They typically require any expropriation to serve a public purpose, such as public health, public safety, or protection of the environment. They also require that the expropriation be accompanied by prompt, adequate, and effective compensation. The following example is taken from Article 6 of the 2012 US Model BIT:

1. Neither Party may expropriate or nationalize a covered investment either directly or indirectly through measures equivalent to expropriation or nationalization ("expropriation"), except:

   (a) for a public purpose;

   (b) in a non-discriminatory manner;

   (c) on payment of prompt, adequate, and effective compensation; and

   (d) in accordance with due process of law and Article 5 [Minimum Standard of Treatment] (1) through (3).

2. The compensation referred to in paragraph 1 (c) shall:

   (a) be paid without delay;

   (b) be equivalent to the fair market value of the expropriated investment immediately before the expropriation took place ("the date of expropriation");

   (c) not reflect any change in value occurring because the intended expropriation had become known earlier; and

   (d) be fully realizable and freely transferable.

Expropriation can take on various forms. The most obvious is direct expropriation through the taking of the ownership of assets by the state. But expropriation can also occur in more subtle ways. Therefore, treaties cover not only acts of direct expropriation, but also indirect forms of expropriation. The latter play a much more important role in practice than direct expropriations. Examples include acts factually depriving the investor of the control of the investment, such as the withdrawal of a license essential to the business, increases in royalties or taxes that render the business unprofitable, or discriminatory subsidies to major competitors that force the foreign investor out of business.

There is no generally accepted definition of indirect expropriation. Whether an act amounts to indirect expropriation can only be determined on a case-by-case basis. The severity of the state's interference is to be considered as well as the duration of the interference. In their assessments, tribunals usually pay attention to the impacts of a state interference and tend to assume indirect expropriation if an investor is deprived of the economic benefits of the investment.

Expropriation does not necessarily need to be the result of a single act or a number of simultaneous acts. Expropriation can also occur in a gradual way. It may, for instance, be the cumulative result of a series of measures implemented over a period of time. There is some debate as to whether temporary measures by a state can constitute an expropriation. While the taking of property for a very limited period of time (e. g. in the context of a seizure) does not necessarily constitute an expropriation, it is widely accepted that the impacts of non-permanent measures may also amount to an expropriation.

Many awards make reference to a formula first used by the tribunal in *Metalclad Corp. v. United Mexican States*:

> "[E]xpropriation under NAFTA includes not only open, deliberate and acknowledged takings of property, such as outright seizure or formal or obligatory transfer of title in favour of the host State, but also covert of incidental interference with the use of property which has the effect of depriving the owner, in whole or in significant part, of the use of reasonably-to-be-expected economic benefit of property even if not necessarily to the obvious benefit of the host State."

There is no general rule to determine at what point a deprivation of the economic benefit of an investment has reached the level of "significance".

Another challenging issue is the determination of an adequate compensation. Treaties hardly provide any guidance on methods for such an assessment. There are a number of different approaches, including methods that try to determine the market value, methods based on the evaluation of assets (book value methods), and variations of discounted cash flow methods.

9. THE STATE HAS TO ACCORD FAIR AND EQUITABLE TREATMENT TO THE INVESTMENT

Nearly all investment treaties include the obligation of the contracting states to accord "fair and equitable treatment" (commonly referred to as "FET") to investors of the other contracting state.

The FET standard is the standard most frequently relied upon in investment disputes. Its scope of application is extremely broad and covers a wide range of discriminatory interferences with a foreign investor's business operations. While there is no unique definition of the term "fair and equitable treatment", two issues have been in the focus of the discussions: the protection of an investor's legitimate expectations and aspects of due process.

FET clauses protect an investor's legitimate expectations, including those regarding the stability and consistency of the host state's conduct within its legal framework. In principle, an investor should be able to rely on the legal framework that exists at the time of the investment. Unexpected changes in the legal regime may amount to a violation of a FET clause. In addition, the investor should be able to rely on assurances given by the host state, be it by way of a specific agreement or in some other form. On the other hand, an investor cannot expect that existing regulations will never change. No doubt, a state has the right to regulate matters and to amend existing regulations and legislation. It is up to the tribunals to strike an appropriate balance between the investor's legitimate expectations and the host state's right to regulate. Prominent recent examples that have led to claims by foreign investors include changes to the regulations concerning feed-in tariffs for renewable energy. Investors in the renewable energy sector had relied on calculations based on tariffs which were arguably guaranteed by the host state. Spain and the Czech Republic, for example, faced a number of claims because of amendments to regulations in that sector after foreign investors had started doing business.

The second essential element of protection under the FET standard relates to the investor's entitlement to fair procedure, whether in court or in administrative matters. Unfair proceedings or even the denial of justice constitute violations of the FET standard. However, it is not the purpose of tribunals in treaty-based arbitrations to act as a super-appellate body by reviewing the state courts' application of substantive domestic law. Rather, it is a disregard of commonly recognized fundamental procedural rules, such as the right to be heard, that is likely to be considered a violation of the FET standard.

Bad faith is not an essential requirement for protection under this standard. In other words, also *bona fide* actions by the host state may represent an unfair or inequitable treatment of an investor.

In many BITs, the FET clauses are complemented by an obligation of the host state to accord "full protection and security" to the investments of nationals of the other contracting state(s). Sometimes, this standard and the FET standard are combined in a single clause. The distinction between the two concepts has remained somewhat unclear. Some tribunals have held that "full protection and security" relates to the failure of a state to take positive action to protect the investment from adverse third-party interference or force majeure, while the FET standard is intended to protect against actions of the state itself. In some instances, tribunals emphasized the element of *physical* protection, while others extended the scope of the "full protection and security" standard beyond the physical integrity of the investment. The first BIT ICSID award dealing with "full protection and security" (*Asian Agricultural v. Sri Lanka*) involved an incident in which Sri Lankan security forces destroyed an investor's shrimp farm and killed some of his employees. The tribunal found that Sri Lanka's failure to take reasonable measures to prevent the incident constituted a violation of the "full protection and security" standard.

10. CONTRACTUAL RIGHTS CAN BE PROTECTED UNDER THE "UMBRELLA" OF INVESTMENT TREATIES

Many BITs contain a provision requiring each contracting state to observe investment obligations entered into with investors. This may become relevant when an investor enters into a contract with the host state or a state entity for a specific project.

For example: A foreign investor has entered into an agreement with the government of the host state about the implementation and operation of an IT-based system for monitoring goods arriving at and departing from a state-owned harbor. The investment agreement provides for disputes to be resolved by litigation before the competent local court. After the system had been in operation for a few months, the government stops making payments to the investor for the services provided.

As an alternative to pursuing claims in local litigation, the investor might be able to institute investor-state arbitration on the basis of a BIT which contains a so-called umbrella clause. Such umbrella clauses, also referred to as "observance of undertakings", "sanctity of contract", or "*pacta sunt servanda*" clauses, may provide the protection of an investor's contractual rights under the "umbrella" of an investment treaty. They typically state that "*each Contracting Party shall observe any obligation it may have entered into with regard to investments of an investor of the other Contracting Party*". Hence, a (simple) breach of contract by a state may, at the same time, constitute a breach of the state's promises given in an investment treaty. This could pave the path for investor-state arbitration.

While some tribunals, commentators, and practitioners reject the idea of the "transformation" of mere breaches of contract into an international wrong by virtue of an umbrella clause, others emphasize the so-called rule of effectiveness, i.e. that all the words and clauses of a legal instrument should be given effect. The latter favor a broad interpretation of umbrella clauses to the effect that such clauses impose treaty liability upon a state for violations of contractual obligations in agreements between the state and an investor. There have been attempts to limit such a broad application of umbrella clauses to instances in which a state has made use of its sovereign or governmental powers, as opposed to the conduct of a normal party to a commercial transaction.

In any event, it is once again important to pay particular attention to the exact wording of the clause. Among the most famous decisions relating to umbrella clauses are the decisions of the tribunals in three different arbitrations instituted by the Swiss company Société Générale de Surveillance S.A. ("SGS"). They deal with three slightly different but still similar umbrella clauses.

The first decision was issued in 2003 in an arbitration against Pakistan based on an umbrella clause in the Switzerland-Pakistan BIT. In that case, the tribunal declined jurisdiction due to the lack of evidence that the parties to the BIT had the intention to transform a violation of a contract into a violation of international law by virtue of the umbrella clause (*SGS v. Pakistan*).

The second decision was rendered in an arbitration against the Philippines in 2004. The tribunal accepted that the umbrella clause in the underlying Switzerland-Philippines BIT could turn a violation of a contract into a violation of the BIT. However, it considered the "*extent of content*" of the obligations under the contract as a matter to be determined by the forum selected in the contract. In other words, it did not feel competent to determine the amount due. Consequently, it stayed the proceedings pending a decision on the amount due by the forum selected in the contract (*SGS v. Philippines*).

The third decision was rendered in an arbitration case against Paraguay in 2012. The tribunal held that the umbrella clause in the BIT between Switzerland and Paraguay provided for protection against breaches of commercial contracts by the host state. Going one step further than the tribunal in *SGS v. Philippines*, it did not consider the forum selection clause in the contract to constitute an obstacle to the admissibility of the claim (*SGS v. Paraguay*).

Meanwhile, there have been a number of other decisions with varying conclusions.

EDITORS & AUTHORS

Jörg Risse

Prof. Dr. Jörg Risse is widely recognized as one of Germany's leading arbitration lawyers. With his dual qualification as an attorney-at-law in Germany and in New York (USA), he represents his clients in international arbitration proceedings under the rules of all major institutions, with a particular focus on M&A-related disputes. Jörg is one of Germany's most-in-demand arbitrators; as a result, his clients also benefit from his "judiciary" outlook on a case. He teaches dispute resolution and advocacy skills at the University of Mannheim and at Humboldt-University, Berlin, and is an experienced, CEDR-accredited mediator.

Heiko Haller

Dr. Heiko Alexander Haller co-chairs Baker McKenzie's German Dispute Resolution Practice Group and is one of Germany's leading arbitration practitioners, both as counsel and arbitrator. He is particularly experienced in disputes relating to large infrastructure, construction and IT projects, as well as in contractual disputes involving pharmaceutical companies. Heiko frequently publishes and lectures on international arbitration topics.

Ragnar Harbst

Dr. Ragnar Harbst is a partner in Baker McKenzie's Dispute Resolution team. He is qualified as Rechtsanwalt in Germany and Solicitor of England & Wales. Ragnar published widely on all aspects of international arbitration, in particular the area of witness evidence. Between 2016 and 2020, he was a co-chair of the ICC Task Force on the Accuracy of Fact Witness Testimony in Arbitration. Ragnar also teaches legal writing at the University of Frankfurt.

Jürgen Schramke

Dr. H.-Jürgen Schramke, a partner in Baker McKenzie's Frankfurt Office, has more than 20 years of experience as counsel in litigation and arbitration proceedings. A particular focus of his practice is on large-volume plant construction and infrastructure projects, including (nuclear) power plants and offshore wind farms. He frequently publishes articles and speaks at conferences on arbitration, adjudication and construction law. Further, he has special expertise in investment arbitration.

AUTHORS

Markus Altenkirch

Dr. Markus Altenkirch joined Baker McKenzie's Dispute Resolution Practice Group in 2012. Since then, he has handled more than 35 international arbitration cases involving mostly post-M&A disputes as well as disputes arising from license and distribution agreements (in particular in the pharmaceutical industry). Markus teaches at the University of Mainz and regularly publishes in the field of international arbitration. He is the editor of Global Arbitration News, Baker McKenzie's blog on international arbitration, and a co-host of zukunft, the German language podcast on the future of arbitration.

Tobias Höfling

Dr. Tobias Höfling is a senior associate who joined Baker McKenzie's Dispute Resolution Practice Group in 2013. Tobias has many years of experience in advising shareholders, companies and their corporate bodies on commercial law, corporate law and post-M&A matters. In addition to representation before state courts and arbitration tribunals, Tobias' practice focuses on out-of-court dispute resolution. Tobias frequently publishes on topics related to international arbitration.

Annette Keilmann

Dr. Annette Keilmann, counsel in Baker McKenzie's Dispute Resolution team, has 14 years of experience in domestic and international commercial litigation and arbitration. Her focus is on disputes in the construction and engineering industry, particularly plant engineering and infrastructure projects. Annette teaches negotiation skills at the University of Mannheim and has published widely on various commercial law and arbitration topics.

Gerrit Niehoff

Dr. Gerrit Niehoff knows both worlds: Having worked in the legal department of a global biotech company on secondment, he combines the pragmatic view of an in-house lawyer with the expertise of an outside arbitration counsel. Gerrit mainly advises on international arbitration matters, with a focus on IP-related disputes and disputes in the healthcare industry. He frequently publishes on topics of international arbitration and litigation.

Max Oehm

Dr. Max Oehm joined Baker McKenzie's Dispute Resolution Practice Group in 2016. He has handled more than 20 international arbitration cases as counsel and served as secretary to tribunals. He concentrates on advising clients on managing risks and resolving disputes relating to professional services, infrastructure projects and post-M&A. Max regularly publishes and presents on topics relating to international arbitration. He teaches negotiation skills at the University of Mannheim.

Maximilian Sattler

Dr. Maximilian Sattler joined Baker McKenzie's Dispute Resolution Practice Group in 2013. As a senior associate, he advises clients across the entire range of commercial law, with a focus on construction disputes (from both the customer's and the contractor's perspective) at all procedural stages. In addition, he has particular expertise in the rapidly developing field of cartel damage claims and all related factual and legal issues. He frequently publishes on topics of commercial law and teaches at the University of Mannheim.